Our Powerful Words

Growing Loving Relationships Through Heartfelt Words

By

Clelia SantaCruz - LMSW

Warren Publishing, Inc.

Text copyright © 2008 by Clelia SantaCruz - LMSW

Warren Publishing, Inc.

All rights reserved. No part of this book may be reproduced or transmitted in any form by any means, electronic or mechanical, including photocopying, recording, or by any information storage system, without permission in writing from the Publisher.

www.Warrenpublishing.net

Several persons mentioned in the text are personal friends or family members of the author and have given permission to use their names, herein. All other resemblances to persons living or dead are purely coincidental.

All Bible verses quoted in this work are from the
New International Version.

ISBN 978-1-886057-23-4

Library of Congress Control Number: 2008941646

Manufactured in the United States of America
First Edition
17039 Kenton Drive Suite 101-B
Cornelius, North Carolina 28031

To my husband, Alex:
When God put us together He knew that
He was taking us to a new level.
Thank you for helping me to grow!
Thank you for making me realize
The things that I was missing in life!

To my sons, Eddie and Josh:
You two are the sunshine in my life.
God blessed me abundantly
when He sent you to me!
Thank you for your love, support and
friendship; without you I couldn't
have made it.

To my mother: Even though the ride was rough
for many years, we finally found each other!
Thank you for believing in me and giving me
the love I always wanted.

To my dad: I learned to laugh because
of you! I learned to cry because of you!
I love your contagious happiness
and incredible charisma!

To my sister Loydette,
for being my best friend!

To my brothers, for loving me
unconditionally!

To my stepson, Gabriel: I am so blessed
to be a part of your family!

To all of my friends who have supported me
and believed in my vision:

Thank you
for listening and being there
when I needed you.

To pastors Dan and Becky Dean,
Sherry and John Ferris,
Jack and Martha Langham,
Shellee Hicks and Barbara:
Thank you for sharing your experiences
and allowing me to tell your story.

Thanks also to my clients:
I hope that during our sessions you
were able to see Christ through me!

To Bishop Jack DeHart and his precious wife Doris
for believing in God's vision to build an orphanage in Nicaragua.
God sent you into my life and I am eternally grateful for your
belief in me and for your help with this assignment.
You have been an incredible blessing in my life.

Contents

Introduction..1
Chapter 1 The Truth that Set Me Free...............................5
Chapter 2 Making an Impact on Others...........................39
Chapter 3 Dealing with Guilt..47
Chapter 4 Our Powerful Words......................................53
Chapter 5 Releasing to God..63
Chapter 6 Letting Go of Resentment...............................67
Chapter 7 Flesh or Spirit..77
Chapter 8 The Laws of the Universe...............................89
Chapter 9 Planting Good Seeds......................................93
Chapter 10 The Law of Attraction..................................97
Chapter 11 Visualizing Intimacy in Your Marriage.........103
Chapter 12 Betrayal..109
Chapter 13 The Paralyzing Power of Fear.....................115
Chapter 14 Ramifications of a Bad Decision.................121
Chapter 15 God Had Other Plans.................................131
Chapter 16 Putting Our Pasts Behind Us......................151
Chapter 17 We Are Special in His Eyes........................157
Chapter 18 Making it Work..163
Chapter 19 Passing the Test..171
Chapter 20 Lustful Desires...179
Chapter 21 Divine Intervention....................................197
Chapter 22 There Are No Accidents.............................205

Our Powerful Words

"I do not understand the mystery of grace--only that it meets us where we are, but does not leave us where it found us."

-Anne LaMott

Introduction

After a painful divorce that left me carrying bitterness and disappointment, God placed in my heart the desire to write about the pain that divorce causes not only to couples, but to children, extended family, and friends. I have had the desire to write a book for many years, but took no steps to do it. The topic of my book kept changing in my mind depending on my circumstances, but even when I finally figured it out, it took me several years to put what I wanted to say into words. After leaving my first husband and experiencing the consequences of my actions, I knew that I had to let couples know the importance of staying together and allowing God to change their hearts and their thoughts about the most important institution established on earth.

A marriage is a covenant that we as couples establish with God and each other. When we face trials and tribulations in our relationship and we make the decision to break our covenant because we have reached an impasse or have a self centered mentality, the words of our Lord Jesus Christ found in Matthew 19:6 should come to our minds, "What therefore God has joined together, let no man put asunder." Remembering that foundational principle can help us turn things over to a higher power. If God sees us as one, we must see our relationship as a union created by God. A house divided cannot stand, and a divided marriage cannot survive. When we ask God for grace and understanding in the midst of a storm, He will give us the strength to make changes, the wisdom to heal the pain, and an opportunity for a new beginning with our significant others. Unfortunately, I did not choose that path, and as a result I caused tremendous pain to people who loved me, my ex-husband, our relatives, and especially my children. If I had walked closer with God and had spent time in His presence each day, I would not have allowed temptations to enter my mind.

Clelia SantaCruz - LMSW

At some point in my hectic life – attending school to obtain a masters degree, working full time, and raising two sons – I lost the connection that I had with my husband as well as my Heavenly Father. I began to look at the world for answers that led me to the wrong path. Satan had a mission to destroy my family and I helped him do it.

The decisions that I made that day have impacted each one of us in different ways. The pain of a shattered marriage left scars that have been difficult to heal, but healing does come when we surrender our pain to God. I have learned from my experiences that family is the most important thing in my life. The things that truly matter have nothing to do with money, education, or power, but include the peace that only God can give, good health, and the love of family and friends. There are times when we selfishly throw away our blessings in search of excitement or something new, and it is not until we lose the blessing that we realize how precious it truly was.

I wrote this book with the intention of reaching couples who are experiencing significant conflict in their relationships and are contemplating divorce. The principles and techniques I write about can be applied to any relationship. It is my hope that this book will inspire its readers to make positive changes in their lives and achieve spiritual, emotional, and physical success. This book can help single people to learn the importance of choosing the right person and being specific about the qualities of a potential mate.

This book is about the importance of having a daily relationship with God, and the tremendous power of our words; what we believe in our hearts and say with our mouths can change the course of our lives. It is also about having faith in Christ and trusting that He can help us in any situation or in any circumstance. It is about love, marriage, and the story of couples who choose different paths in search of a solution to their troubled marriages.

After pain and disappointment, many couples turn to God and allow healing to take place. Some couples end their marriage because they can no longer handle an abusive relationship. Other couples end their relationship in search of passion and excitement. As a result of poor decisions, some of us break a covenant that we made with Christ and each other. Matthew 6: 13-15 states, "Wide is the gate and broad is the road that leads to destruction and many enter through it. But small is the gate and narrow the road that leads to life and only a few find it." I left the broad road of destruction and by His grace found the narrow road back to Him – where I am choosing to stay. I can't change my past or erase the pain that I caused to my family and myself, but I can use my experience and the experiences of the couples who chose to share their stories in this book to help people who are seeking answers about their personal relationships, and to glorify my Lord Jesus Christ.

    I begin this book by writing about the changes that God has made in my life and how He can use anyone to carry out His purpose. I had the desire to write books many years prior to my most recent encounter with God. I gave my life to Christ over twenty years ago, but it has taken many years for Him to reach me and take me to a place where I can fulfill my purpose. Several years ago, He completely changed my life; He began by changing my heart. My old desires radically changed direction. Today my goal is to reach people for Christ! He has led me to places that I never thought I would go and to do things that I never thought I would do. The last chapter of this book is about the God-sized assignment that He has placed in my life.

    If you have experienced pain from decisions made in your past or if you are considering ending your current relationship, it is my hope that this book will help you work through your pain and find comfort in the hands of God. My desire is to help you learn techniques to enhance your life and acquire a love for Christ that can fill the voids in your life.

    Upon the completion of my manuscript, I sent certain chapters to my siblings so that they would know that I have written about our family and my experiences. Some of my family members did not agree with me exposing our "family secrets" and I could certainly understand how it was offensive to them. But I don't want any secrets in my life and what I write about is my experience, my truth. I don't write my truth to hurt anyone, my writing has to do with the experiences that I have gone through and what God has done for me. It was said that I am attacking Hispanic men and our values and traditions. I do not mean to attack Hispanic men or Hispanic culture. My intention is to tell my story and help those who have gone through similar experiences.

Our Powerful Words

"The great gift of family life is to be intimately acquainted with people you might never have even introduced yourself to had life not done it for you."

-Kendall Hailey

"One of the secrets of a fruitful life is to forgive Everybody, everything, every night before you go to bed."

-Bernard Baruch

Chapter One

The Truth That Set Me Free

It seems that some of us are born into perfect families, or at least we believe our families are perfect until we compare them to others. I always knew that my family was different, but that somehow I had been placed there for a reason. It has taken time to realize that God has a purpose for each one of us and that He places us where we need to be. Our lives take turns that are difficult to comprehend. For those of us who believe in destiny, our lives take the turns that they are supposed to take. We may impact the results temporarily by our daily decisions, but eventually we will reach our destination. I understand today that growing up with my family made me the person who I am today. God has given me many opportunities for growth and even though I still question the difficult situations in which I sometimes find myself, I know that He is right there cheering me on to the finish line. He has been preparing me and slowly molding me for the next spiritual level.

It took me many years to get to a place where gratefulness became a part of me. I am so thankful to God for everything that He has given me. When I learned the secret of gratefulness, I truly began to exist. No longer did I think of what I was missing. No longer did I have time to feel sorry for myself or desire what others had. Instead I began to appreciate the wonderful blessings that God had given me.

Clelia SantaCruz - LMSW

I love my family and have a perfect understanding of each and every member, but I could not have gotten here without the love of Christ and the power of prayer. Prayer completely changed my life because it allowed me to get to know God intimately. Knowing Christ changed my heart, and therefore everything around me was also changed.

I was born in a small, beautiful, and safe town in Nicaragua where most people knew each other. Our family consisted of my father, my mother, myself, and two older brothers. My father was a medical doctor whom everyone – except my mother – seemed to love and respect. I attended Catholic private school for twelve years, and with that came generations of traditions and expectations that I did not understand. I saw my mother go to church daily to ask God for the same thing, but the miracle that she appeared to be praying for never came. She believed, like many Catholics at the time, that she had to offer sacrifices to God and to the saints in order to have the answer to her prayers, which I am sure at the time, was about her horrible marriage.

My father was extremely unfaithful, insatiable when it came to women. It was almost impossible to keep maids working for us because he would become sexually involved with them. Night after night, he would wait for my mother to go to sleep and then sneak into the maid's room to seduce her. Some of the maids would even become pregnant! My mother found out about his infidelity through different sources. Sometimes it would be very obvious – like when a maid who supposedly did not have a boyfriend would become pregnant. Or sometimes a particular patient would come to see him everyday and spend too much time in his office. Other times, people would inform her that they had seen him with a woman somewhere. When it came to the maids, my mother was hyper vigilant and at times paranoid, watching their every move.

My father had his private practice but also worked in the local hospital where he was surrounded by nurses who found him attractive and could not say no to his seductions. Rumors about his unfaithfulness would reach my mother, but she did not know half of what was going on at the time. When my mother found out about each of these relationships, she would become suicidal – and homicidal.

After many years of feeling completely disrespected by her husband and suffering from her own childhood issues, my mother developed a deep depression that kept her from enjoying life and giving her children the nurture and love that we so desperately needed. I grew up with a mother who was unhappy, angry, and depressed. I did not understand my mother's pain and anger until much later.

I remember, when I was about nine years old, sitting outside my mother's bedroom one day waiting for her to pull the trigger of her 38 revolver. I remember banging my head on the wall and thinking, "Just do it, please just do it. Get it over with…I can't take this anymore." I had witnessed her depression and her suicidal behavior so many times that I was scared, but completely tired of it. She would go into her bedroom and pray, but her temptation to end her life was incredible. She was miserable and did not know how to deal with the pain that she was experiencing. She kept the revolver in her nightstand and would take it out often, always praying and fighting the desire to kill herself. I never knew if she was going to do it or not, and not knowing if she was serious that day or the next was torture. Seeing her incredible anger, depression, and pain was confusing for a child my age, and I learned to hate her because I could never please her and make her happy.

I loved my father; he could always make me laugh by telling me stories that he made up. He was sweet and attentive to me when he had time, which was not very often. As a child, I craved love but love from my parents was scarce to say the least. At the time I did not know all of the particulars about my father's insatiable desire for women. I only knew that my mother was unhappy, depressed, and angry at everything and everybody.

My mother had grown up in a terribly dysfunctional family. When she was a small child, her father died and left her mother a widow at twenty-five with five children. Grandmother did not have a nurturing spirit, and her children grew up neglected and abused. My mother never learned how to express her emotions. She never learned how to love because no one gave her love therefore it was difficult for her to show love to her own children.

I remember dinnertime being the worst time in my house; there would be an argument almost every night. Mother could not stand being around father, and anything that came out of his mouth would offend her. His mere presence upset her. I remember not being able to eat because the chaos upset me so. To this day, if I am in the middle of eating and conflict of any kind erupts, I immediately push my food away, unable to take another bite.

Seated at the dinner table, my father would look at us as if my mother were crazy and would make faces as if to say, "I am innocent. What is she talking about this time?" He would tell us that my mother was losing her mind. For a long time, I believed his lies and thought that she was actually demented. I did not realize that he was actually *driving* her crazy with his infidelity and denials. In the middle of dinner, she would go to her room, slamming her bedroom door. We would not see her until the next morning, when she would wake in a horrible mood, screaming at the servants and especially at me. I remember waking up many times and praying to God that mother would be in a good mood, but my prayers were never answered!

Our maids did not last very long, not only because of my father's seductions, but because they could not put up with my mother's abusive language and incredible demands. She had an obsessive compulsive personality and everything had to be perfect. At times, they would all just quit and we were left with no maids or maybe just one. I would have to do some of the housework but I never did anything right in her eyes. She had a way of making me feel completely inept and worthless. She would make me mop the floor over and over and it never looked good enough. Finally, after years of witnessing her depression, my father sent my mother to a psychiatrist hoping he would prescribe shock treatments. My father thought that the treatment would erase some of her memories. He thought that if she did not remember all his infidelities, then maybe she would not be mad at him all the time. The psychiatrist did not think that she needed shock treatment and instead he just pumped her up with drugs so that she was heavily medicated most of the time. Her depression continued, and her anger did not go away.

Not knowing what to do to alleviate her depression, my mother's psychiatrist prescribed pregnancy. He thought that having another child would occupy her mind and time and bring some kind of joy in her life. My mother followed his advice, and my sister, Loydette, was born when I was nine years old. After giving birth, my mother must have experienced a bad case of the blues – the prescription did not work. Things got worse instead of better! It appeared to me that my mother was more miserable than before, although some days she seemed to enjoy my new sister. I am sure that Loydette brought my mother some joy, but her depression and anger seemed to have her under control and the joy from her small child could not fully alleviate her symptoms.

As my sister grew up, the little attention that I had received from my father was diverted to her, and I grew up resenting Loydette. Not only did I have to take care of her, but she was also a spoiled brat who told my parents everything that I did. When she was seven, they began to send her on dates with me because they knew that she would immediately describe all the details of my evening. My boyfriends would have to buy her gifts and do whatever she wanted to keep her quiet.

Today Loydette is a beautiful woman who loves God, and is a great mother and my best friend. I am so thankful that she was prescribed because she has brought joy into my life, and we will always have each other.

I believe that my mother was depressed not only because of the external issues she was dealing with – being married to an unfaithful man and coming from an extremely dysfunctional family – but also because she had allowed Satan to come into our home with her desire to contact the dead. As a physician, my father was a man of science and believed in nothing else but science. My mother, on the other hand, dabbled in many other things like tarot cards, bringing mediums into our home and trying to obtain physical healing from witch doctors. There were nights when a medium would come to our house at midnight to conduct a séance or contact the dead. My mother yearned to get in touch with her father and to feel his presence since he had been killed when she was so young. Some of her friends would come over to join the séance and hear from their loved ones who had passed away. I was maybe ten or eleven years old and would hide somewhere in the next room, trying to see what was taking place. It was both scary and exciting to watch the medium transform before my eyes.

As a teenager, I became increasingly interested in finding answers about life, and for a while I became absorbed with the mysteries of the afterlife. I always have had a gift of persuasion and was able to talk people into doing anything I wanted them to do, positive or negative. I would talk my friends into going to the cemetery and playing with the Ouija board on top of someone's grave. I wanted answers and believed that dead people or Spirits could give them to me.

As an adult, I have noticed more and more how sensitive I am to the Spirit realm. It is a difficult subject to explain to others because unless they have experienced the spiritual world, they do not comprehend what I am saying. I believe that God has given me the Spirit of Discernment, and I treasure it because it has allowed me to experience situations that normally I would not have experienced otherwise.

When we look for Satan, it does not take long to find him. I know now that like my mother, I opened many doors for him and it has taken knowing my rights as a Christian to renounce and break those curses and other curses that came from my ancestors.

Isaiah (NIV) 65:7 states, "I will pay back into their laps both your sins and the sins of your fathers." I don't take that lightly; I believe that there are things happening in our lives that we don't understand, strongholds that have not been broken. Until we break those curses from our past, we will not be able to have a successful life. We must know our rights in Christ. We are children of God, and He has redeemed us from the curse of the law, but we have to claim our blessings and renounce Satan from our path.

In spite of all of her frustrations, my mother allowed the sweet Spirit of God into her life. She had a giving heart and would daily feed the elderly begging in the streets. She would also visit the local prison and bring the inmates a nice, home-cooked meal. Seeing that side of my mother was confusing to me, because what I saw at home was her bitterness, unhappiness, regret, and at times plain hatefulness. I grew up confused about the mixed messages that my parents sent me and allowed a rebellious spirit to enter my heart at an early age. I did not want anyone to tell me what to do and would try to get into trouble just to get attention. I also became depressed and at the age of thirteen I wanted to kill myself because I felt unworthy. I felt that I did not belong anywhere and that there would be no big loss if I were to end my life. I wanted to be perfect so that my parents and siblings could love me, but I did not know how to be. I was angry at the world and I was angry with myself.

I remember being afraid of killing myself. I wanted to do it, but did not know what method to use. I knew that I did not want to blow my brains out because I had been so afraid of my mother doing it. I thought about taking pills since we had all kinds around the house. My father's clinic was located in the home and therefore I had easy access to all of his sample medications, but by the grace of God I never took any pills nor acted upon my desire.

I spent numerous hours writing poetry, but my poetry depressed me even more; I wrote only about death. God uses our experiences so that we can help others. Years later when I worked in psychiatric hospitals and saw so many kids write about sadness and death, I could relate to them and help them. There is a reason why we go through experiences. We may question for years why certain things happened in our lives, but one day it becomes clear that we are here to help others.

I don't know what became of all of the poems that I wrote. I wish that I could find them now to see how truly dysfunctional I was at that time. I know that God was watching over me because I survived that stage of my life. Through His guidance, I ended up impacting others in a positive way with my profession. I don't understand how God has been able to bless me after all of the screwed-up decisions that I have made in my life. His love has sustained me throughout the years.

At the age of thirteen, I began to date one of my brother's friends who was five years older than me. He seemed to love me (that is what he called it) and always wanted to be around me. I decided that if I married him, then my problems would end. He was finishing high school and going away to college. We dated for about a year before his parents sent him abroad to study. God had other plans for me, but at the time marriage to my first boyfriend had seemed right.

Time passed, and I continued to try to figure out who I was and I was failing miserably. To others, though, I appeared to have it all together. My mother's critical comments made me believe that there was something wrong with me. I could never measure up! I know today that she had received the same messages from her own mother. She did not know how to be a part of my world or let me be a part of hers. Her messages were very confusing to me because I felt accepted by others – especially boys.

As a teenager, the messages that I received from boys meant everything to me; boys made me feel pretty and desirable. I had lots of friends and was popular in school so I could not understand why my mother hated me so much. I could not have possibly known then that she hated herself and not me! I felt as is she were my enemy and I was always on the alert, waiting for her attacks. I wanted to get back at her for the way that she made me feel, so I did many things to provoke her.

Many afternoons after school, I would come home, then leave again, just to be away from my house. I enjoyed hanging out at the lumber-yard near our house. I have always been fascinated by ants, and I would spend a lot of time watching them carry food and follow what seemed to me at the time to be some type of order. I felt as if I were the god of the ants, knowing exactly which turn they were going to make. I

Destiny?

Our Powerful Words

would take the food that they were carrying on their backs and put it somewhere else. They would act crazy then go back, find it, and carry it again! I would place roadblocks in their way, but somehow they would always find their original path. I remember wondering, "Is this the way that God can see us?" I would imagine that He was this huge human being watching us and placing things in our path just to see where we would go and how we could handle the challenge.

If you watch an ant going a certain direction and then build a small mountain to keep it from its path, the ant will go around or climb it, and will reach her destination sooner or later. That is the way that it should be with us! When interferences appear in our lives, we should be able to go around or climb them in order to get to our destiny. But I was a lost child and my destiny was extremely unclear at that time.

In our town, there were two private schools -- a girls' school that I attended, which was run by nuns, and a boys' school run by priests. I was going into the tenth grade and the boy's school announced that year that they had decided to become co-ed. I was extremely excited about the possibility to get out of the school I was attending and begged my parents to enroll me in the co-ed school. The opportunity to be around boys was great because during my entire existence, I had attended an all girls' school. Public school had not been an option, as my parents would not allow me to attend due to our "sick society rules." People of a certain social class should not be mixed with others. That type of thinking created the revolution and civil war that we later experienced as a country. I applied and was accepted to the private co-ed school and I quickly began to date a boy in my class. My first boyfriend had gone away to college, and even though I'd had intentions of waiting for him to return, I enjoyed dating too much to sit around and wait. My new boyfriend, Raul, was the tallest guy in town, which was great because I was the tallest girl in town and had felt awkward about my height. Nicaraguan people are not supposed to be tall, and I wondered how in the world I ended up taller than anyone else. Today I am proud of my five-foot, eight-inch stature. That's not much around here, but back home it was a problem. Raul and I became inseparable and dated for about three years. I only lasted one year in the co-ed school. I was

13

having too much fun sitting at the back of the classroom with all of the boys and not paying attention to the subject being taught by the priests.

One of the priests liked me to sit in front of the class right by him. The minute that he came into the classroom he would say, "Clelia to the front." I hated to sit so close to him because he spit so much when he spoke! One day I brought a small umbrella, and as he began to teach I opened it up. When he asked what in the world I was doing, I told him that I was tired of getting my hair and face wet from his spit and that an umbrella would protect me from it. Not appreciating my honesty, he sent me home! That little incident started a negative experience that lasted the entire year, so the next year I returned to the nuns. The priests were tougher than the nuns and the classes harder. I liked to do enough work to just barely get by and I accomplished this well. Actually, it did not matter what kind of grades I brought home because my brother was a straight A student and I could never measure up. I remember my father telling me how stupid I was for not understanding math and that he wondered how could I be so different from my brainy brother.

I did not like the nuns who ran our private school and I wanted nothing to do with religion. The nuns were quite abusive, but of course at the time I could not see that my behavior had anything to do with the way that they treated me—today I am quite sure that my behavior was the reason! Religion was part of our everyday curriculum at school and Sunday Mass attendance was required. I remember being forced to go to church every Sunday and getting nothing out of it but fear and shame. I could not wait to graduate from high school and choose a school away from all of that tradition and confusion – and away from my miserable parents.

I did not understand the presentation on the Holy Spirit during services. At some point during the services, the Holy Spirit was brought out in a beautiful little box. When He was out, we were supposed to close our eyes as a sign of respect. After communion, He would be back in the box, and we would not see Him again until the next Sunday. Eventually I came to realize that the Holy Spirit is with me every minute of the day and not in some box waiting to be let out.

Our Powerful Words

I knew about Jesus and I had seen people pray to Him for different reasons. I prayed to Him at times, but I did not spend much time praying to saints like the rest of the Catholics who I knew. I never thought that saints could hear me, but everyone else around me had their favorite saint who would come to their rescue whenever they asked. Back then I did not understand the power of prayer. I did not know that God could bring me out of my horrible experience and give me peace. Today I understand that God knew me before I was in my mother's womb. He knew everything about me and He still chose to place me in the household in which I grew up. Why? To this date I don't know, but I believe that it was to help others who feel lost and lonely like I did back then.

My experience as a child has shaped who I am today. Bad decisions that I have made in my life are part of the experience that I am supposed to have. God knew how much I was going to mess up, but I think that He hoped I would make different decisions. Many times I had the opportunity to choose the right thing. Due to fear that was masked as different emotions, I made decisions that I thought were the best at the time and ignored the Holy Spirit who was right by my side, trying to get my attention. I was an unhappy kid and I was terrified for anyone to know. I pretended that I was tough when the truth was that I was just scared to death inside. God knew how I felt, and all of these years He has been slowly shaping me, removing the veil from my eyes, and showing me His love. If we need a way out, then He can show us the way, but we must spend time in His word and in His presence in order to know His voice.

When I was growing up, we were not encouraged to understand the Bible; actually I don't even remember if we were allowed to read it. We were made to believe that only priests could understand the word of God. I don't know if they thought that we lay people were just plain dumb and that God could not speak to us without the involvement of a priest. Today I am so glad to know that Jesus did not come to give us religion, but to have an intimate relationship with us!

Clelia SantaCruz - LMSW

We had three priests in our town, two of them were wonderful, but one was known to practice communion too much! He really enjoyed the wine part. Weekly confession was a tough thing for me; having to tell the priest about my sins after I saw him drunk the day before was difficult. During the required, or what I called "forced," confession, I usually just made up stuff. I could never tell the priest all of the things that I was doing. I believed that they probably would have thrown me out of the school and the church and given me a penance to say prayers for weeks in order to cleanse me of my sins. I was rebellious and got into trouble often. I began drinking alcohol at an early age and was angry when my parents tried to discipline me. How could they tell me what to do when their own lives were such a joke? I had no patience with anyone and could act just as hateful as my mother.

Once I got tired of waiting on the school bus for the bus driver. I blew the horn several times and when he did not come, I became extremely impatient. I asked everyone if they wanted to go for a ride. Those who did not want to get in trouble with the nuns got off the bus, the rest stayed, and I drove the bus off campus. When I got back, Mother Superior was waiting for me and punished me severely by forcing me to mop the floors of the entire school for days. She suspended me for two weeks, but luckily my parents never found out because my mother was out of town and my father was too busy. In the mornings, I would get up and act as if I were going to school and no one knew the difference.

My mother traveled often from Nicaragua to California and Texas to shop, especially when she was depressed. My father was usually busy with his practice, his ranches, and his women. I am sure that he loved when she went away for several weeks because he was free to do whatever he wanted.

For a few years, we had a maid named Esmeralda, a saint who put up with my mother's moods. I remember begging her not to ever leave because she was my lifesaver. She seemed to love me, something foreign in my life. I felt so unworthy – my parents did not want me and my brothers hated me. Esmeralda cared for me and would protect me from my brothers, especially the one who was the most abusive. She would also take care of my indiscretions by covering for me. If there were calls from school, she would answer them as if she were my mother and the nuns never knew the difference. I loved that woman! I often think of her and wish that I could see her again. No one knows what became of her, but one day I know I will see her again and thank her for the love that she showed me.

Partying and having fun was my way of escaping from my troubles. I broke as many rules as I could break. If we had a field trip, it was a wonderful opportunity to persuade some of my schoolmates to leave the group and find some kind of trouble to get into. My favorite field trips were those that would take us out of the city; I would travel to another city in the school bus with everyone else, but on the return trip I liked to hitchhike back to town, something that I found fascinating. Eventually due to my trouble-making, I was not allowed to participate in some of the school activities, but since my parents never knew what was going on, I would tell them that I was going on a school trip. This allowed me opportunities to do what I wanted to do and hang out in places where I should not have been. I was able to manipulate my situation in such a way that I eventually regained my school privileges.

I left Nicaragua at the age of seventeen, right after high school graduation. My parents had wanted to send me to Europe, but I feared going to a country where I did not know anyone. I convinced them to let me come to the United States to learn English. California and Texas were places that I had visited during school breaks. My parents had allowed me to come to this country on my own to visit relatives and go wardrobe shopping since I was fourteen.

During the trip after graduation, I met a man who was seven years my senior named Eddie who drove a beautiful convertible. Back home, European and Japanese cars dominated the market so I fell in love with Eddie's American car! He was a wonderful guy and spoke a little Spanish so we communicated most of the time by guessing. I was so excited that an older guy was giving me so much attention. Eddie said that God had showed him a girl like me in a dream. He believed that I was supposed to be his wife. God did not speak to me at all in those days, mainly because I did not speak to Him, and therefore I did not know or understand what Eddie was saying. We dated for a couple of months until my Visa expired and I returned to my country, sad to leave Eddie behind.

I had been dating Raul back home for over three years and he was very happy to know that I was coming home. When I got home, he started to talk about marriage, and my parents feared that if they did not send me back to the United States or to Europe, then I would end up marrying Raul, which was totally unacceptable to them. They wanted me to become educated and see the world. Since I was terrified to go to Europe by myself, they sent me to Massachusetts. Texas was not a choice because they knew that I had met Eddie there and they were trying to get me away from men in general. My parents wanted me to learn English and said that the North offered better English than the South. I could not understand where they got that idea. However, I was happy to be anywhere in America, thinking that it would be so easy to get to Texas. Geography was not my best subject, and I did not realize that traveling from Massachusetts to Texas was almost as far as going from Massachusetts to Nicaragua.

Massachusetts turned out to be a nightmare, and it wasn't just because of my geography problem. The climate was totally different from what I was used to in sunny Nicaragua, so I spent four months freezing to death. It didn't help that I arrived in the dead of winter. But the biggest problem was that I was thousands of miles away from my home and did not speak English. Back home, I could talk to anybody – even a rock, in Spanish, of course. But here I almost turned into a mute. I did not pick up the language as easily as my parents had hoped that I would. Still, the language barrier didn't prevent me from getting into trouble my very first week in Massachusetts.

My first experience in Massachusetts was in Boston where I lived with a family who had two daughters and one son. I never knew what I did to cause the lady of the house such dislike for me, but it was a sad time in my life. Her husband and her son liked me and probably enjoyed looking at my seventeen-year-old, voluptuous body. Mary, as I remember her name to be, became jealous of the attention that I was receiving from them. I spent one week with this family before being thrown out of the house with no explanation. I was thousands of miles away from my home and did not speak the language. It was the scariest time of my life and I knew no one who could help me.

My problems with that family had all started one night when I was supposed to go out with the youngest daughter, Lisa, to a school dance. Lisa was fourteen years old and I certainly did not want to hang out with kids that age. The oldest daughter, Terri, who was eighteen years of age, had invited me to a different kind of party. Somehow I understood "party," but had difficulty with every other word in English. Terri made a deal with Lisa that I would leave the house with her, acting as if we were going to the little, nerdy, junior-high party. Instead I would go to the "fun" party with Terri and then she would drop me off at the school prior to her mother picking us up. It sounded perfect, but it wasn't. To my wonderful luck, a water pipe broke in one of the bathrooms and the school flooded. The party ended at a much earlier time than expected. Of course, cell phones did not exist and there was no way for Lisa to let Terri know of such disaster.

When Terri dropped me off at the school, the lights were off, the party was over, and someone told her what happened. I understand today what happened, but back then I had no idea what was going on. Terri was scared of her parents and did not want to get in trouble. She left me at the school and one of the boys who were with us dropped me off at the house. Mary was waiting for me and when she heard a car, she immediately went outside, armed with a broom. The boy was about to get out of the car and explain to her what happened, but she began to attack him before he could say anything. The boy ran off and left me there with the woman who had gone mad. She pushed me into the house, saying things that to this date I would not want to understand. I could not defend myself and could not say that I had been with Terri. She pushed me upstairs and began to pack my clothes in my suitcase. I remember crying the rest of the night, not knowing what I was going to do.

Clelia SantaCruz - LMSW

Around 6:00 A.M., Mary got me up, took me to the bus station, and put me on a bus. She gave me a piece of paper with some address and left me there. I was petrified! I could not ask any questions because I did not know how and no one spoke Spanish. The bus took off, apparently for another city. When it came to a stop, people got out and I was the only person left on the bus. When I saw my suitcase outside, I decided that I needed to get off because maybe that was my destination. When I saw no one come for me, I began to panic and I knew that I was lost. I sat on my suitcase and had begun to cry when an African American man came to me and asked me something. I did not know what he said, but I showed him the address on the paper that Mary had given me. He grabbed me and grabbed my suitcase and I was terrified, not knowing where he was taking me. He took me to another side of the station and put me on another bus. I had not finished sitting down when the bus took off. I remember looking at that man and saying "thank you." I know today that he was an angel sent from heaven and I never forgot his face.

I ended up in Three Rivers, Massachusetts with a family who had one son in prison, one son in the army, and an girl who had a horrendous bird that flew all over the house and dropped his waste everywhere. She wanted to learn Spanish and their intention of having me there was so that I could help her practice. My parents had paid good money so that I could learn English, and therefore I felt as if somehow I was being used. The family turned out to be nice, but completely different than what I was used to. Meals were not cooked in that house, they certainly did not have maids, and I didn't even know how to boil water. I was in trouble! Potato chips became my best friends and I also discovered tortilla chips. I had grown up eating tortillas, but never in the form of chips. I fell completely in love with them and along with potato chips they were my constant companions. Gaining a few pounds was shocking, because I had been thin my whole life.

I felt as if my entire world was changing and I was not very happy in United States. I knew that my parents had paid thousands of dollars for "the wonderful experience." I did not know what to do because I did not want to go back home and be around my parents and all of their problems, but I was miserable in Massachusetts. I was also afraid of wasting all of the money they had spent on me because they had had a similar experience with my oldest brother.

My brother had been sent to Argentina to study medicine, and after my parents had paid for one year of education and room and board, he decided that he was not staying there. He hitchhiked his way back to Nicaragua, losing the money my parents had invested in his education. After he got back from Argentina, both of my brothers were sent to Mexico to a private university called La Salle. I knew the kind of money that my parents were spending on education alone. I did not want to waste their money and hear them complain about it. They were also going through a divorce, and the last thing that I wanted was to be in the middle of it.

I spent four agonizing months in Three Rivers eating potato and tortilla chips and fighting with the dreadful bird who flew all over the house. Not only did he drop his waste everywhere, he was also very aggressive. According to the people from my country who placed students in the United States (and were obviously running a scam), I was supposed to attend a school of languages. There was no school of languages; they put me back in high school with kids who I did not care to be with. I had already graduated and it was a nightmare going back to high school after being out of it for almost one year. Not one girl liked me, I stood out like a sore thumb, and I could see hate in those girls' eyes. The guys were friendly to me and I had no problem talking to them with my extremely limited English, but I did not make one single girl friend. They used to call me the "Raquel Welch of Three Rivers," but not in a loving or nice way! (I guess now you can guess my age.) I dreaded going to school every morning and I thought that I was in hell – but questioned it because it was too cold.

I could not stand being in Massachusetts any longer and one day I called Eddie to come to see me. When I dated him in Texas, he had asked me to marry him, saying that he had a vision from God about me. I asked him if he still wanted to marry me, he said "yes" and came up

Clelia SantaCruz - LMSW

with the money to buy me a beautiful ring. He came to Three Rivers and we were married.

We returned to Texas where I could see my relatives, but soon after our wedding, I became confused. I was lonely and I wanted to go back home. Eddie worked long hours and I was left in a small apartment with no car and no one to talk to. I missed my family, even though there was nothing there but sadness. Sadness was familiar to me and life in the States had turned out to be pretty much a nightmare. I was still having difficulty with learning English, so I had difficulty expressing myself, and I was lonely, scared, and depressed. Eddie was the manager of a clothing store in a local mall and some mornings I would tell him to take me with him, even though I knew that I was going to have to spend the day there because he worked twelve hours days. When I went with him, I would go to the stores to shop, but quickly realized that I did not have any money. I couldn't just buy stuff at stores and tell them to bill my parents like I did back home.

My dad refused to talk to me; he had become ill after finding out about my wedding. He was extremely upset about my decision to marry someone from another country. I had not consulted him and that broke his heart. One day before Eddie came to get me, I had called home and announced that I was getting married. I remember my father asking me if I were crazy and asking who I was marrying. I told him I was marrying the guy who used to call me every time we sat down to dinner back home. After I had left Texas, I went back home and Eddie would call often to talk to me, but for some reason, he would call when we were eating dinner and my father had a big issue with it. My parents had begged me not to marry Eddie and asked me to come home, but it was too late, Eddie was on his way and I wanted to be a grown up and get married and do my own thing. I remember saying, "I am going to be free." That by itself was crazy; we are never free by getting married.

After I married Eddie, my parents quit sending me money and I did not know how valuable money was until I lost it. Going shopping just to look was not fun! Eddie felt sorry for me; I was sad, bored, and broke. He tried to make it better by giving me a credit card! I thought that was the most wonderful thing, it was better than the tortilla chips that I had discovered in Massachusetts. I would be so happy to give that thing to the clerk, knowing that I did not have to have money to shop. We never had credit cards in Nicaragua. When my parents bought anything including cars or homes, they paid cash; there was no such little, plastic thingy.

My days were spent waiting for Eddie to come home so that I could talk to someone or going with him and trying to amuse myself somehow. I don't know why he would not let me drive him to work and keep the car. I had been driving in my country since the age of thirteen and I drove a beautiful BMW that I shared with my mother and here I didn't even have a car.

At some point, my parents forgave me for marrying so young. They had other plans for me; they wanted me to marry someone chosen by them or at least someone whose family they knew. ==My mother came to Texas to see me right after our wedding and she was actually loving and understanding.== My father, on the other hand, never wrote or called. More than one year passed without my father speaking to me and after hearing from my mother-in-law, Lupe, that I was depressed and that I needed help, my father finally came. Lupe was a wonderful woman who loved God and loved me as if I were her own child. My father decided to forgive me for my "unspeakable act." He made me promise that I would not marry Eddie through the church (being the strong Catholic that he was... actually he only went to church for funerals and weddings). At that time we were married only by the court. He also made me promise that I would not get pregnant, but I was already pregnant with the most beautiful little boy who would bring tremendous joy into my life.

My child, Eddie, – who has made my life complete – had just been conceived, but I did not tell my father that piece of information for fear that he would again become ill or get mad at me. My father met my husband and his family and seemed to like everyone. He could see that they were good people and felt that they were treating me well. He came to love Eddie very much, although he could never say his name right. To our surprise my sister, Loydette, married a man named Eddie and they also had a child who they named Eddie.

My father came and left and my life continued to lack something. My desire to return home did not go away, but that was no longer a choice. I had given birth to a precious little boy who needed to be near his father and I could not take him away from his father even though the thought entered my mind many times. But traces of my option to return home quickly faded because Nicaragua began to have political issues. The civil war started and the rebels took over the country, turning it into a nightmare. Communists from Germany and Cuba made their presence and took up residency and everything changed forever. Now I could not go back home. Even though my culture would not have accepted a divorced woman at the time, I had been willing to take that chance. But that option was forever gone and it depressed me even more.

One day I got up and decided to make the best of my situation. I made the decision that I was going to master the English language and I was going to attend school. I took English as a second language and began to watch soap operas in order to force myself to understand the language. If I wanted to know what was happening in Pine Valley, then I had to understand English. Therefore I would pay attention to everything. I would practice my English with little Eddie. He was so precious and cute; he spoke his English with a Hispanic accent even though he did not speak Spanish. Since I was trying to learn English, I failed to speak to him in Spanish and robbed him of learning a beautiful language that would be of such benefit to him today.

I was fascinated with psychology and decided that studying it would help me understand my dysfunctional childhood. I remember taking one of my first psychology classes; it was a psychoanalysis class where our teacher had us practice exercises to get in touch with our past. I thought I had it all together! In my mind, being angry with my parents had served me because I became tough and aggressive and that protected me from others. I did not take anything from anyone and was quick to defend myself against any perceived injustice. When our teacher started asking questions about our parents, my repressed emotions came flowing

Our Powerful Words

out like a broken dam and to my surprise I was overwhelmed with pain. I could not stop crying and felt embarrassed to show such emotion. I began to grieve for the confused little girl who had wanted her parents' love and acceptance, but had never gotten it.

With all of the emotions of my past and the problems I was having in my marriage, I became even emptier. After six years of marriage, I continued to be unhappy. I had a void in my life and often felt sad, even though I had a wonderful husband and a precious, little boy who had enough energy to make the whole state of Texas light up.

My husband, along with some extended family members, began to pray for me to find God and fill the void I had in my heart. Sometimes they prayed so much that they would scare me. Eddie sometimes would say things like, "Satan, I rebuke you in the name of Jesus," – as he was talking to me! I remember saying, "What are you doing? Have you lost your mind? I am not the devil!" I did not know that he desperately wanted the Spirit of conflict to leave our home. After much praying and having holy water thrown at me, I finally opened my heart to receive from God.

I remember being by myself one day and lying down on my bed, crying about my life. I was feeling terribly empty inside when I heard a noise that got my attention. As I looked up toward my dresser, I could see the pages of my Bible move. It freaked me out and I started looking around and feeling for a draft that might be coming into the bedroom. I knew that the wind must have moved the pages, because no one was home with me. Slowly I walked toward the Bible and I could almost hear an audible voice saying, "Read my word." I felt overwhelmed and did not know if it was fear or joy. I began to read the Word and a few weeks later, I gave my life to Christ. I don't know why my first experience with God was dramatic. Not everyone experiences God in such a way and I would never want to give the impression that God had to do something out of the ordinary to get my attention as if I were special. Your personal experience with God might be different! All I know is that He desires for each and every one of us to come to Him and we are all special in His eyes.

Soon after that experience, I decided to make my marriage work and began to entertain the thought of conceiving another child, because that might make me happy. I did not know that I was as fertile as Nicaraguan soil and a few months later, I got pregnant again with my youngest child. The emptiness that I had experienced had somehow lifted and I was so excited about having a precious child in my womb. I would talk to my baby and sometimes read her stories. I could not wait for her to be born. Seven and one half months later I gave birth to a precious little boy whom we named Joshua. He was born prematurely and he was supposed to be a girl. The doctor had informed us that it was a girl and I had everything pink in preparation for the daughter I always wanted. God had other plans, and the little girl who I thought I was having turned out to be a boy who I now adore with all of my heart.

Joshua has been the most wonderful gift that God could ever give me. Both of my boys are true gifts from heaven. They have never given me any significant problem – other than that each has a heavy right foot wrapped with lead and they love to financially support every city that they pass by acquiring traffic tickets. Other than wasting lots of money on city improvements, Eddie and Josh have been respectful and loving with hearts made of gold. The lead in Eddie's foot was surgically removed a few years ago and he has not had one speeding ticket in the last few years. Josh apparently has something heavier than lead in his right foot, but we are working toward resolution on that matter.

My life was good for many years and actually, prior to our divorce, Eddie and I were the happiest that we had been. We decided to buy a bigger house and fell in love with an older home and moved in with no problems. I believe that house had inexplicable powers. The original owners ended up divorced and as a result sold the house. The owners who we purchased the house from spent their time away from each other and were experiencing difficulties. I never knew if their marriage ended in divorce. I believe that there was a curse in that house and we failed to cover our family with the blood of Christ.

Our Powerful Words

After a year of living there, I again began to feel as if I were missing something. I spent time with God, reading His word, and I was scared to experience that horrible emptiness. I could experience God's love, but somehow it wasn't enough. Looking back, I know that I failed by just reading the word, but not meditating on it. I busied myself with raising children, attending school, and working. I quit praying and spending time in His presence and soon after, I allowed negative thoughts to enter and occupy my mind.

While working on my graduate degree, I became completely out of touch with my marriage. I was too busy trying to graduate and doing everything else – including working outside my home. I did not need to work, Eddie was very successful in his business, but my desire to make it on my own was bigger than my desire to take care of my family. To add to our issues, Eddie began to experience incredible pain in his hips, and after an incident where his legs gave out at the age of forty-five, he underwent double hip replacement surgery. It was a very difficult time in our lives. While he was lying in a hospital bed, I was trying to write my thesis, work full time, and take care of Josh. Our son, Eddie, was about to graduate from high school and Josh was very involved in sports and needed to be taken to practices and to school. I have been told that Eddie felt as if I did not do my part in taking care of him while he was recovering from such tough surgery. Maybe I didn't, but there were too many things going on at the time. After weeks of recuperation, Eddie finally got better, but our problems just continued.

Eddie and I grew further and further apart and one day, after a big argument where I finally realized that I was not going to be used by him any longer, I decided to end my marriage. In my heart I believed that my children would be happier if my husband and I were apart from each other because then they could see us smile. Apparently I thought that I could not smile anymore if I stayed in the marriage! I asked Eddie to leave our house and told him that I wanted a divorce. The lies that Satan had put in my mind had become real and I believed that the only way out was through divorce. I felt that it was my time and that I had wasted too many years being unhappy. Any time we begin to think in terms of "me, me, and me," we should pay attention to where that voice is coming from. Our flesh and our Spirit are the complete opposite of each other and when we are living a life for Christ, the temptations to destroy a covenant blessed by God becomes more and more enticing because Satan is working full-time against us and his mission is to destroy families.

At the time of our separation, our son, little Eddie as we called him, had just graduated from high school and therefore I thought that it would not affect him in a significant way. How wrong I was; the consequences of divorce affect children at any age. At eighteen, Eddie had a very difficult time seeing his family destroyed. Watching his parents fighting with each other and seeing everything that he had known change over night was something that he should not have to have gone through. I remember as if it were yesterday when he looked into my eyes and told me that it was fine if I wanted to leave his dad. He said that he just wanted to see me smile again because somehow I had lost my joy. My son, Eddie, and I have always been extremely close and he sacrificed his feelings to let me know that he would always love me, no matter what decision I made in my life. He placed me first before his feelings and for that I will always be grateful. What a gift from God that child has been. Everyone who knows Eddie or Josh can see the gift that I was given when God gave them to me. I have been truly blessed to have them in my life.

We never know what our children are thinking; we never know what details they are paying attention to or what is going through their minds. We are wrapped up in ourselves and can think of nothing else but our own misery, disregarding our children's misery. We fail to protect them and forget to ask about their feelings when it should be our number one priority to do the best with the precious gift that God trusted us with.

Josh was pulled in all directions and his reserved personality made it impossible for him to express his feelings. He began to experience stomach problems at his young age and our separation impacted him tremendously. He was eleven years old when his dad and I separated and I still remember his sad, little face when he saw his father move out of the house. My husband was extremely hurt by my decision and he began to fight me for Josh's custody and that was the most painful part! Eddie's attorney was dragging me through the mud. He was trying to prove that I was not a good mother based on abuse that I went through as a child. He brought up issues from my past, saying that I had been sexually abused and therefore I was mentally unstable. I felt as if someone were piercing my heart with a knife. During my marriage to Eddie, while working on my Master's degree and taking clinical classes, I began to have memories of sexual abuse. I became extremely confused about facts and blamed the wrong people for things that were done to me as a child.

When I was eight years old, my friends and I used to go to my neighbor's home to play. He was an old man who lived with his mute daughter. They had all kinds of fruit trees in their huge back yard, and it had great hiding places. We could play hide and seek all afternoon and it would be a wonderful time. We did not care about playing with his daughter because she could not speak, but we loved the back yard and visited often. The man touched me inappropriately many times and at that age I did not know how to react. I knew that I disliked it, but it was the price to pay to hang out in his back yard. Many times he touched me in front of his daughter, but she could never say anything because she was mute. I remember looking into her eyes and seeing panic, and panic is what she saw in mine. I believe that he was sexually abusing her, too, and when she saw him touch me, she hurt for me.

That girl's face tormented me for many years and I never did anything about it. One day, after many incidents where the old man fondled me, I told my father. He prohibited me to go to that house, but nothing else happened! I hoped that my father would kill him, but he did not. He did not say anything to him and I felt as if he did not care about me. I was very hurt and angry and never told him anything else that happened to me because it would not do any good anyway.

Later that same year, a family friend began to take me out to eat, to buy me candy, and do other "fun" things. This man had three sons and no daughters and when he began to pay attention to me, everyone thought that he was treating me like the daughter he never had. I always wondered why his wife never said anything. My mother would allow me to go with him everywhere and never questioned his intentions. Why would a grown man want to hang out with a small child all the time? To this date, I don't have all of the memories of his abuse; all I know is that I was terrified when the memories started to invade my life. After being terrified, I became extremely angry for what he did to me and for having parents who did not question his intentions and who had failed to protect me from him. Since I had so many issues with my mother, I blamed her the most. I asked myself how she could allow that to happen to me. Today I know that it was not her fault. She did not know that someone who lived next door and appeared sane could be so evil.

Several other incidents happened in my life and I conquered each one of them by myself. I was all alone and I could not ask for help because I knew that no one was going to help me. I guess that I put all that behind me for many years, until one day everything came out to the light and I did not know what to do with the pain. I was very angry about my past and did not know how to deal with the anger.

Eddie did not know what to do because I couldn't even speak about it. He assumed that my father had abused me and used that against me in court. He was wrong because I never accused my father! I remember sitting in the attorney's office, fighting to keep my child and having to answer for things that I should have never had to defend myself for. Eddie was in a corner of the room, apparently praying in the Spirit. I always wondered how someone could pray in the Spirit and hurt someone else so much at the same time.

That incident set me back! I had tried to put my past behind me and I did not know how to stop the pain. Until one day, I put it all on the altar and asked my Heavenly Father to heal my heart because I could not stand the pain. He took my pain that day, but the pain continued to surface. Apparently I was borrowing it back. Later I understood that when we release something to Him, we must leave it there. The minute that we start to think about our problem and tell it to others, we have just taken it from the altar and placed it back into our hearts. God then crosses His arms and waits for us to truly release it. When the thoughts or the pain come back, we have the power to dismiss it and not entertain it in our mind. We can gently say, "I am not taking this pain back, it is gone because Jesus has taken it from me." We must visualize giving our pain to God and leaving it there where it belongs.

Eddie has apologized for the bad experience! It was a bad time for all of us; I have forgiven him for it and he has forgiving me for the part that I played. His attorney could not prove that I was not a good mother based on being sexually abused as a young child. My children had always been first in my life. Josh and I were extremely close and he would have suffered being away from me. After months and months of litigation, the judge decided that I was to have custody of Josh. I might have won that battle, but we all lost the war; the pain of a shattered marriage has lingered for many years and will impact our next generation.

Our divorce caused tremendous pain to those who loved us. Eddie and I had grown far apart and the expectations that we had of each other were completely unrealistic, but it was nothing that God and our desire to work it out could not have fixed. At the time I felt that I could no longer stay in that kind of marriage and felt unappreciated and abused. I did not know that love was a choice; I was led completely by my flesh and ignored the covenant that I had made with God and with Eddie. He fought hard to keep the marriage intact, but I would not listen and did not allow God to work in our situation. Looking back today, I am amazed to see how hard my heart was at that time. I did not have an ounce of compassion because I only thought of myself and my selfish desires. I could see the pain that I was causing, but did not care. God has changed my heart today and I don't ever want to be that kind of person again.

At the time I must have believed that the decision that I was making was the right one, because God had not intervened and I had not been hit by lightning. He did not come down from heaven to stop me from making a mistake and hurting those I loved. I failed to see that He is a gentleman and has given us free will to do what we want to do.

Even when He intervenes on our behalf, many times we are too busy and self absorbed to notice His presence. I remember praying, but I was confused about what I thought I was hearing from God.

The consequences of my decisions were obvious to me later when I saw the pain in my children's faces. It became clear that my actions hurt the people who I love the most in this world. Today, I have no idea how to erase their pain or fix the changes that will impact the next generations, but God is merciful. He has given me wonderful children who love me and respect me and, most importantly, who love God.

Josh and I lived in the cursed house for about five years. (Inexplicable things have continued to happen in that house to this day, but that is another book!) We moved out of the house in 2002, when my current husband and I got married. I rented the home to a couple who, after experiencing inexplicable things, asked me if the house was haunted. Much prayer has been invested in that house and I believe that protection from evil should be something that we pray for on a daily basis.

Years have passed since that day when I felt that I no longer could be married. Today I am still reminded that my actions forever changed the lives of my children, the precious gifts that God trusted me with. I failed Him and I have paid for my decision. I can still see the pain in their eyes and it tears up my heart.

My purpose for writing about relationships is to make a difference in even just one person who is experiencing a similar situation. Maybe through the reading of this book, I can touch his or her heart so that he or she can make a different choice. It is not about us! It is not about our selfish desires, it should be about the commitment and the covenant that we made. It should be about doing the best that we can do with the lives of precious children who God has blessed us and trusted us with, so that they can learn through our actions and imitate our ways.

Our Powerful Words

Eddie has remarried to a good, Christian woman who loves him the way that he deserves to be loved and who is good to my children. Eddie continues to be a strong, committed Christian and God has blessed him abundantly. We communicate about our kids and have a good relationship with each other, which has been positive for our sons. I continue to see Eddie's family and to this date consider them part of my family. Apparently they feel the same about me.

Some members of Eddie's family are like treasures in heaven especially his mother, Lupe, who was like the mother who I felt that I never had. She loved me and accepted me for who I was. Even when I spoke negatively about her son, she would not judge me; she accepted me unconditionally. Lupe died two years after her son and I divorced. Eddie and I had been married for twenty-two years and I believe that our divorce and other deep disappointments in her life contributed to her losing the battle against cancer. I know that Lupe is in heaven; I sense her presence in my life. A couple of years ago, I woke up one morning and somehow she immediately came to my mind and I sensed her presence. I asked if she was in my bedroom and told her that I loved her! When I went to my office and noticed the date, I realized that it was her birthday and I knew for sure that her spirit somehow had been in my room earlier. The pain that I caused her still saddens me, even though I know that God has forgiven me. I wait for the day that I can see her in heaven and tell her what a positive influence she was in my life and what joy she gave me by showing me unconditional love.

God has blessed me again! He has reminded me that He forgives me for my sins and apparently continues to forgive me on a daily basis. I have remarried to a man named Alex who is my best friend! We do not always act like we are best friends, but we have the capacity to be. As I began to write this book about relationships and the power of our words, Satan immediately launched a tremendous attack on my marriage. Many times I have felt completely exhausted from the fight and many times I have questioned my decision to marry again. Toward the end of my writing, gathering last pieces of information, and getting my book ready to publish, I felt exhausted from my marital issues. One morning I prayed and asked the Lord to help me see things the way that He sees them; I thought that I had reached the end of my rope. I asked Him to help me to see Alex like He sees him, because He and I were miles away on that one!

I have prayed the same prayer many times before about different things and He has allowed me to see differently when I truly desire to see things His way. I do not always have that desire because I know that He will change my heart. Then I will be the one saying that I am sorry and many times I want others to say it first, especially Alex! After praying that day, I believe that God showed me the scripture in 1 Timothy 1:5-7 which states, "The goal of this command is love, which comes from a pure heart and a good conscience and a sincere faith. Some have wandered away from these and turned to meaningless talk. They want to be teachers of the law, but they do not know what they are talking about or what they confidently affirm." I thought, "Wow slap me in the face, why don't you!" That was definitely a word for me! Here I am talking about the laws of God throughout this book and yet, during Satan's attacks, I began to give in to meaningless talk. I certainly was not seeing Alex with love! I didn't even like him much less love him. The Bible tells us that love comes from a pure heart, a good conscience, and sincere faith. Apparently I had failed that test! I have no business talking about the power of our words and turning things over to Christ when I am not practicing the law of love, but boy it is difficult!

When we are praying about a situation and want answers from above and then see that our spouse is not trying, it makes us want to give up. He or she might be trying in their own way, but if it is different than our way, we don't consider it right. God has talked to me many times about paying attention to the way that I deal with things and about letting Him deal with the other person because there is nothing that I can do to change anyone else. I have to begin with me. After going through the same lesson over and over, I have realized that it does get easier to practice love and turn things over to God.

I believe that God placed Alex in my life, even though at the time when we married, I did not consult The Holy Spirit the way I would today. Today I would spend time praying and fasting for an answer to a decision that would impact the rest of my life. How foolish it is that many times we make decisions in our lives without consulting the Holy Spirit who is there for us. The similarities in Alex's life and mine are many and I believe that there are no coincidences, although at times I wonder if God just wants to torture us. My husband and I are too much alike and sometimes the clashing can be powerful. At times I feel that God was laughing when he put us together, but no doubt it was God. He must have said, "You are asking for change, let me show you your mirror! What you want to change in him is what you must work on changing in yourself."

My marriage to Alex has been great and it has been difficult. I still have days where I want to walk away and I can see that we are both exhausted trying to see who would give in first because we can both be hardheaded and proud. But when I spend time with the Holy Spirit, He has a way of making me see the light. He knows that my desire is to please Him. My relationship with Jesus has become so much closer in the last five years. As I said before, I did not consult Him before getting into a second marriage. What a mistake that can be, because if God is not involved in our decisions, then we can get into another negative situation and begin to feel that void in our heart. I have found that when I am not walking in the center of God's will, the void that I have experienced most of my life will occupy part of my heart again. Today I know that every decision that I make concerning my life or my children's lives has to involve God. I can't make any decisions; I can't choose what is right without the Holy Spirit guiding my every step. The hardest lesson in my life has been to let go and quit controlling everything around me. I wish that I would get it sooner sometimes instead of fighting every step of the way, but there is hope; I really desire to do God's will. Whatever happens in my life I know that I will serve Him and this time I won't leave Him.

Alex also divorced a godly woman and the pain that he caused his son is still fresh in his mind. She has also gone on with her life and was able to find a godly, loving husband who places her first in his life. We have all taken different paths and know that God has plans for each one of us. I know that my personal goal is to serve Him! My prayer is that He continues placing in my path the opportunities to share His love with others.

My relationship with my mother has improved tremendously. These past few years we have seen each other a lot more because I have traveled to Nicaragua more often. God placed a vision in my heart to open up an orphanage. He also gave me the desire to feed the "forgotten elderly" who reside in asylums with very little support from the government. My mother has traveled with me all over Nicaragua to look for land to build the orphanage and we have spent lots of time together. (For more information about the vision please read the last chapter of this book.) Today I see her with different eyes and have a new love for her and an understanding for the way she deals with issues. No one ever gave her any love and she never learned how to trust others. At times I look at her as if she were a child trying to survive in a cruel world. My daily prayer is that God would place in her life someone that can bring her closer to Him so that she can experience the healing that she so desperately needs.

My father is eighty six years of age and every time I see him it is a gift from above. He is still full of life, but at his age I never know if it will be the last time. I visit him every year and travel several hours from my mother's house to his ranch located in the north of the country. My father has never been able to express emotions other than when he is having an alcoholic beverage. He is funny, loving and energetic when under the influence and that is when I usually get some affection from him. He will hug me in a playful way and will tell me long stories that make me laugh.

One evening during my last trip, we sat around and talked forever under a beautiful sky full of bright stars. I was returning home to Texas a couple of days later and was staying thirty minutes away at my brother's home. He did not want me to drive in the dark and said that it was too dangerous for a woman to be alone on the road. I had stayed at the ranch before, but this time, I did not mean to stay that long and I did not have any of my personal belongings, therefore I decided to drive back to the city.

Our Powerful Words

My father realized that he could not change my mind and invited me to return to the ranch the next morning and promised that he would take me to a place to eat my favorite breakfast. I was very happy for the opportunity to spend more time with him and I woke up early the next day to drive back to the ranch.

I arrived early the next morning to see his workers milk the cows, which I used to love as a child. My father greeted me as if I were intruding on his already busy day. I asked if we were going to eat breakfast and he said that he did not have time. I reminded him that he promised and I felt like a little girl asking Daddy to spend time with her. I quickly remembered that I was no longer a child and that if he did not want to go eat breakfast, then there was nothing that I could do. I reminded him that I was going back to Texas and that I did not know when I could see him again. He did not say much and I gave him a big hug and told him how much I loved him. I waited for him to respond and say the same, but he did not say anything. He made his usual gesture as if to say, "I do too" without saying a word! I looked into his eyes and I said, "I need to hear you say that you love me." I had never heard my father say those words to me and for some reason I needed to hear them that day.

He continued to be silent and I felt very awkward. I walked toward my car and got in it thinking, "I cannot believe how difficult it is for him to express feelings if he is not under the influence of alcohol." I rolled my window down to give him an opportunity to say the words that I so desperately wanted to hear. He could not say them! I wanted to scream and say, "You are such a loser."

Tears rolled down my eyes as I drove away and I wanted to understand why a forty some year old woman would care so much about those three words. I had lived my entire life without hearing them from either one of my parents and wondered why it was so important to hear them now.

Clelia SantaCruz - LMSW

During my drive to my brother's house, I realized that the pain that I felt was probably as intense as the pain that he felt for not being able to tell me. My father never learned to express feelings and therefore could never give us children the validation that we needed from him. I have had difficulty in my own life expressing feelings and emotions, and I hope my children know how much they are loved. It has been difficult to trust in earthly parents who could never tell me that they loved me. It has been difficult to trust in a God who I have never seen; but when Jesus came into my heart, I learned that by faith I can do everything!

I know that one day I will see my father and my mother in heaven and I believe that we will be able to embrace each other and hug and laugh and express our love without the heaviness of the pain that our experiences have caused. Meanwhile I will accept them and love them the way that they are on this earth. I believe that I have learned the lesson that I was supposed to learn when God placed me in their household!

Our Powerful Words

"We either make ourselves happy or miserable. The amount of work is the same."

-Carlos Castaneda

"The game of life is like the game of boomerangs. Our thoughts, deeds and words return to us sooner or later, with astounding accuracy."

-Florence Shin

Chapter 2

Making an Impact on Others

Decisions that we have made in our past seem to impact our present. Our words and our actions are like seeds that we plant in the ground; they produce whatever fruit we planted at the time. I know that I have planted some foolish seeds in my life and the fruits of my errors have had a way of catching up with me.

I was at the grocery store not too long ago and I ran into Pastor Dale. I had met Pastor Dale years ago when he was the headmaster of Covenant Christian Academy where my sons, Eddie and Josh, had attended school.

It was 1985 and I had just given birth to my youngest son, Joshua. My husband, Eddie, had won a trip to Hawaii and we were supposed to go with people from his work. I felt that this was bad timing because Joshua was only two months old; he was tiny and precious and leaving him was extremely difficult. I knew that my son, Eddie, would have a wonderful time being spoiled by his grandmother and aunt, however, I was not sure that I could leave my brand new baby. But Eddie's sister, Geni, had volunteered to take care of the children and I trusted her completely, so we decided to go.

Clelia SantaCruz - LMSW

We left for Hawaii and had a wonderful time, but after seven days away from my sons I was very anxious to come back to them. When we got home, I was exhausted from the trip. Josh woke up every three hours for his feeding and did not seem to care that I was exhausted! It seemed that he woke up more than usual that night.

The next day I woke up to the alarm clock that let me know that it was time to get little Eddie ready for school. I got up and made his lunch as I did a thousand times before, but this time was different because I was still very tired. Eddie was a precious little boy who talked more than he needed to at any opportunity. The school that he attended, Covenant Christian Academy, required its applicants to undergo several interviews before they could be accepted. At that time, you needed a referral from someone associated with the school in order to be considered for an interview. You also had to profess your faith as a follower of Christ. We had all of the right qualifications and had passed the test, so our son had been accepted the prior year.

That morning I packed little Eddie's lunch and drove him to school, hoping that I could get back home, do some of my chores, and, at some point that morning, take a nap while the baby slept. I was able to do just that until the phone woke me up around eleven o'clock. The phone call was from Eddie's teacher, Kathy McCord. She let me know that in Eddie's lunch she had found a Tecate beer – not the Coke that I had meant to pack. They had looked the same in the refrigerator as they both came in red cans.

Apparently Eddie had opened the beer, taken a sip, and screamed to the whole class, "My mom gave me a beer!" I hope he didn't ask for a lime! The teacher had immediately come over to see what was going on, and to her amazement there was a nice, cold Tecate beer sitting next to my son's lunch box. When I heard what had happened, I was speechless... I could not believe that I had done such thing! The teacher proceeded to tell me that we could not send our children to school with alcohol. She knew me fairly well, so I think she was trying to make me feel guilty as if the whole incident was not bad enough. Of course I tried to make excuses, but how do you excuse something like that? What kind of mother was I? The entire school found out and I thought that I would never live it down. I heard about it for weeks! Some people thought that it was hilarious, while others looked at me as if I were a poor excuse not only for a mother, but for a Christian, as well. It was probably the most embarrassing moment of my life and I never wanted to show my face at that school again, but I had to!

After twenty years I thought that everyone had forgotten the horrible incident, but apparently they hadn't. When I saw Pastor Dale at the grocery store what do you think was the first thing that he mentioned? You got it! We laughed at the beer incident and I could not believe that something like that had followed me all these years.

Apparently the things that we do and the things that we say can live forever. I want to be remembered for the good things that I have done and said, but even today, I continue to say things that I should not say and to do things that I should not do. I have one of those personalities that is direct, decisive, and demanding and too often I say what is on my mind while disregarding the Holy Spirit's nudge that tells me to watch it. The people in my life accept me and know that I will say what comes to mind even though I might regret it later. Praise God that I am still under His construction, but I have made many mistakes in my life and have failed to recognize that life has given back to me what I have given to it.

I wasted many years trying to fulfill my desires and feeling bad because I had not made the right choices. For many years, I tried to gain fulfillment from another human being who had no idea how to meet my needs because he could not express his own needs. I finally realized that it was not his job to fulfill my needs, because no one can! I have to accept responsibility for my actions and figure out what I can do to change my negative behaviors. My actions had consequences that I did not want to accept, but whether or not I accepted them, they were there and I was left wondering why things were turning out that way. I later figured out that if I can change my attitude about life and accept responsibility for my actions, then the negative experiences that I have endured can be a wonderful teaching tool. I can apply what I have learned to help others and myself. The bad experiences don't need to be anchors holding me hostage under deep water.

I can choose to be alive or I can choose to be buried with my past. Jesus said, "No one who put his hand to the plow and looks back is fit for service in the kingdom of God." He wants us to leave the past behind and concentrate on our present and on a future filled with His promises. His blessings are waiting, but He won't send them via air, train, or car, we must become aware of his promises by spending time in His word and allowing Him to reveal what His purpose is for our lives. The process might feel slow and sometimes painful, but He wants us to develop character and integrity, and developing those qualities takes time. We must have a grateful heart for the blessing that God has given us. When we look at our lives and notice the good things that we have received, we have no time to concentrate on the negative aspects of them.

I had no clue what I wanted to do with my life until I was in my late twenties. Having two children at a young age should have put me on the fast track to maturity, but it did not. I knew I wanted to go to school because everyone in my family was educated and it was expected of me. At age twenty-eight, after modeling for several years and later failing miserably at owning my own business, I realized my desire to be a medical doctor like my father. I guess I was a little late because a counselor at the University of Texas in Arlington talked me out of medical school due to my age. I believed his words instead of following my heart and I opted for the next best thing – psychology.

I was married and had two small children and did not have a variety of choices for universities. UTA was one of the few choices that I had, and that particular school did not offer a degree in clinical psychology, so I chose social work. After completing my Bachelor's, I went to work as a probation officer supervising juvenile offenders. I continued studying and obtained a Master of Science degree. I then decided to leave the juvenile probation department to do independent practice and work with adult sexual offenders, court ordered anger management cases, drug addicted individuals, and workman's compensation patients.

After years of working with this type of clientele, I suffered a "burnout" and it became clear to me that I could not help people unless they wanted help. Most of the clients that I counseled were court ordered, felt forced to attend the session, and were unwilling to make personal changes. Discussing spiritual issues was inappropriate and I had a difficult time not talking about God. I wanted my clients to know the connection between spirit, mind, and body, and they just wanted to get their certificate of completion without learning anything.

In 2004, I decided to quit counseling clients whom I could not impact spiritually, and my clientele was reduced tremendously. I was at a good place financially to take time off to write this book and decided that it would take me one year to do it, but I was wrong! It has taken me several long years to complete and it has been more difficult than I could have ever imagined. During the writing of this book, I felt a tremendous attack from Satan. As I began to research the topics in this book, I began to experience shame, guilt, and undesirable emotions. It all came from the guilt of ending my relationship with Eddie, the father of my children.

There were weeks where I could not write at all because I felt unhappy in my current marriage, and I questioned if I had made the right decision in marrying Alex. I knew that the decision I had made years ago to end my first marriage was wrong even though at the time it felt right. Eddie and I had tried to get back together three times after our separation, but I had no desire to make it work. I believed that God had given me a new opportunity when I married my second husband, and I did not want to live with regrets.

Having a good marriage takes hard work as well as commitment. Within our first year of marriage, it seemed that all of the devils in hell had come against us. Satan makes it his mission to destroy marriages because they are symbolic of the relationship between Christ and the church. It seemed that he was working overtime to destroy ours. I questioned how I could write a book about relationships when the temptation of ending my second marriage was beginning to enter my mind. I thought about leaving my husband and not looking back. I asked myself, "Why not?" I had already divorced my first husband, the father of my children. Second marriages are easier to leave behind, especially when the union has not produced children. Statistics show that most second marriages end within two years. We divorce our first husbands, marry a second one soon after, and then think, "What did I do? Why did I rush into this?" Many of us feel that we have wasted time in our pasts, and that if things are not going to work out with our second spouse, we might as well end it now instead of wasting more time with someone who is not going to make us happy. What we don't realize is that the problems we had in the past are our issues and if we have not resolved those issues, they will surface again in our next relationship. Happiness is a choice, no one person can make us happy because happiness is a personal journey. If we go into a relationship expecting someone to fill that need, they will fail us every time.

It is amazing how we choose to ignore obvious signs during the dating period. We meet someone and think that they have the qualifications that we are looking for in a mate. But do they really? Could it be that we just have a need to belong and that we rush into marriage thinking that we are more mature and that this time we know how to handle conflict? Let's face it, we are going to have conflict in every relationship because we are marrying another imperfect human being like ourselves.

Second marriages are extremely difficult when we rush into them soon after divorce. Statistics show that step-parents will help raise 50% of children under the age of eighteen. Statistics also show that divorce affects boys more than girls and that it will impact their lives for many years. The pain caused by divorce will affect many generations. Seeing the effect that my divorce had on myself and on my family has helped me to see the importance of writing and speaking against divorce and the breaking up of families.

In my personal experience, it has not been easy to live with someone who has a completely different parenting style than mine.

Our Powerful Words

Many times I wondered if our intentions were the same, and I tended to get defensive when my husband told me how to deal with my own children. Discipline issues caused division between us and I was constantly reminded of the consequences of my actions.

    The Bible tells us that we wrestle not against flesh and blood, but against principalities in darkness. Satan will attack us with temptations and thoughts that will keep us from enjoying the blessings of God. It is up to us to stand up against his darts. Satan does not attack me with worry or depression, but he knows what a fool I am when it comes to guilt. I tell my clients that guilt is a useless emotion that can drain the life out of us, so it is funny that I did not recognize it in myself. God sometimes uses people – strangers or acquaintances – to help us see the truth.

    I attended a committee meeting for our church one Saturday and I actually dreaded participating in the long meeting that we had planned for that day. The committee wanted to spend some quality bonding time together in order to create the synergy necessary to come up with ideas that could help the women in our church. As I drove to the meeting, I sensed heaviness in my heart and began to pray. I did not know what I was praying about, but I prayed in the Spirit the whole way there.

    Some of the women in our committee were people whom I admired and liked. One of them was my pastor's wife and I felt that I could trust her completely. I had interviewed her for this book and felt that I knew her in a special way. The rest of them were acquaintances and I did not feel very comfortable around some of them. After a wonderful prayer and a feeling of the presence of the Holy Spirit, two of the ladies informed me that they had been experiencing negative feelings toward me. One of them said that she wanted to get to know me but felt that, "I thought I was so much better than her." Obviously she had sensed something negative about me and somehow I had unintentionally made her feel unwelcome in my world. I took their comments to heart, which showed me how much I had grown in Christ because normally I would not have accepted negative comments that way. The old Clelia would have said, "Forget it, I could care less how you feel about me," I had been so criticized by my mother for so many years, that did not feel I could take it from anyone else and I probably would have left the meeting. I could not do that this time because I felt that the presence of God was so real that He had to be a part of my healing process. They began to ask me what was going on in my life and could sense that my spirit was heavy with pain. I don't like to discuss my personal issues with people who are not close friends, but somehow I had so much pain inside me that I began to tell them that I was experiencing problems in my marriage, and that I could not continue to carry the guilt of divorce and the pain that I had caused my family. I don't know if my pain had caused me to not give my all to the committee or to act as if I were better than them, but the outcome of sharing my concerns with them was incredible. These women began to pray over me and it was a wonderful healing moment. I experienced complete freedom and felt the weight come off my shoulders.

"I gain strength, courage and confidence by every experience in which I must stop and look fear in the face…I say to myself, I've lived through this and can take the next thing that comes along."

-Eleanor Roosevelt

"Your three best doctors are faith, time and patience."

-Unknown

Chapter 3

Dealing with Guilt

While experiencing problems in my marriage, I looked for their root but could not find it; the root of my problems was hidden under a tremendous amount of confusion. The guilt of breaking a covenant that I had made with God and my ex-husband was causing emotions that I could not identify. I found myself comparing Alex to my ex-husband. I compared all kinds of things, punishing myself to remind myself that I had made a mistake; that way I could make sense of the guilt that I had been carrying for so long.

On my way back from church one day, God reminded me that I have a habit of holding on to guilt. My guilt issues began many years ago. My mother made all of her kids feel guilty for existing! She told us that if it had not been for us, she would have never stayed with my father and allowed him to ruin her life. She said that if it had not been for us, she would have moved to the States with her sisters and would have been happier!

Now that I am aware of the guilt trip that we were subjected to as children, it is easy to understand why my sister and brother are so easily manipulated and made to feel guilty. I knew that I could make my little sister feel guilty with just a few words. Even as a grown up, I still enjoyed making her feel guilty and making fun of her weaknesses! I would make comments to her that would remind her of something and then laugh about it when she began to show signs of guilt. I would tell her that she was dumb for feeling that way, but bless her heart, she did not know any better and I was just being cruel to dig into her exposed areas of pain.

I never understood why my oldest brother did not feel any guilt, until I realized that he had drowned his guilt with alcohol to the point that he could not feel anymore! When he came up for fresh air, which was not very often, we could see a glimpse of the beautiful person that he was, but he could not stay sober long enough to commit to anyone. He lost his first family, married again, and continued to be a poor excuse for a father and a husband until God finally healed him two years ago.

I carried so much guilt for so many years, that I felt as if the weight of the world was on my shoulders. I was responsible for everything!

When I met and married my first husband at the age of eighteen, I had been dating my high school sweetheart back home whom I had promised to marry. After finishing high school at the age of seventeen, I left my country and came to the States. I met my ex-husband, Eddie, and after dating him for a few months, I married him knowing that the boy who I had dated for three years loved me very much and trusted me to come back to him. Based on the poor decisions that he made after finding out that I married someone else, I know that I broke his heart and destroyed his hope. Years passed and everyday I thought of him and had dreams about him. People who knew him would tell me that he suffered so much because of me. I was no longer in love with him, but I was not free of him because I was a slave to my own guilt and emotions. I felt guilty about my decision for over twenty-four years!

I felt guilt again when I married my current husband. I could not forgive myself for causing Eddie pain and disappointment. I could not forgive myself for hurting my children and my entire family. I had prayed about the guilt several times and apparently would give it up only to borrow it right back. It was not until that day when a group of women prayed for me and two of them expressed negative feelings towards me that I opened and received their prayer. Many times God will use people or circumstances that we would not normally use in order to minister to us. We must realize that in order to receive healing and blessings from God, we must be open-minded. There are angels disguised among us.

I have a client who for many years has allowed guilt and fear to rob her of the peace that God desires to give to her. Satan has used the guilt weapon to keep her in binds. Lori is a wonderful woman with a heart of gold. She has cheated herself from the blessings of God and has not been able to move forward in her life because regrets from her past occupy her mind on a regular basis. Lori divorced her husband after ten years of marriage and she believes that the ripple effect of divorcing the father of her child did not stop with her, but has affected others in ways that she never imagined were possible. Her marriage was not a good one because she married a man who could not offer her the qualities that she was searching for in a man. But at that time, like many of us, she had no idea what qualities were important in order to have a successful marriage. Marriage was not important to her husband! After the wedding, he continued acting as if he were single, but he expected her to act like a married woman and fulfill every one of his fantasies and desires. At times he would drink excessively and would abuse her mentally and emotionally.

Lori was unhappy for many years, but she stayed with her husband because she wanted to offer her children security and a two-parent household. The marriage produced one child and she also had a son from a previous relationship. Both children have suffered the consequences of her actions and she has had to carry the guilt of her decision. Lori has been divorced for twelve years and she feels that ending her marriage was selfish. At the time, she concentrated solely on the misery that she felt and she denied the positive aspects of her relationship. Her husband failed to give her the priority in his life that she felt she deserved. She felt lonely and neglected – feelings that were familiar to her because they reflected the relationship that she had had with her father.

Clelia SantaCruz - LMSW

As we grow up, we tend to attract people who have the characteristics of our guardians. Lori's father ran his house with as much rigidity as a boot camp. In his mind, he wanted to raise strong and independent children, thus showing love and affection would have interfered with his goals. Her father was a compassionate man when it came to other people, but somehow that compassion did not translate with his children, especially Lori who fought him at every opportunity.

Lori could not wait to get out of her father's house, and when she left at age seventeen, she was instantly attracted to a man who displayed the same characteristics as her father. She married a man who subconsciously reminded her of him. She had tried to get away from the negative treatment that she received as a child, but found herself in the same situation. Her husband was not emotionally available and challenged her just like her father had in the past. She sought approval from her husband, approval she had never received from her father. After several years of marriage, his behavior had made her very unhappy and she finally made the decision to leave and not look back. As with her father, she could not wait to get her husband out of her life to search for what she thought would make her happy. But it did not come. She continued to attract and become attracted to men who could not provide what she so desperately needed – validation. She needed to feel special, appreciated, and loved. Not knowing how to find a man who offered these things, she opted for men who were emotionally unavailable and kept ending up with "bad boys."

Years have passed, and looking back Lori knows that she could have asked God to heal her marriage, and thereby found the validation that she desperately needed. Her ex-husband has mellowed, he has ceased his excessive drinking, and years of dealing with the consequences of his actions have made him see life in a different way. Lori has a good relationship with her ex-husband because she wants her daughter to experience peace in her life, but the decision that she made years ago continues to haunt her to this day. She believes that if she had not been self-centered but rather God-centered, her life would have turned out differently. Her children have gone on with their lives, but the pain of Lori's divorce lingers, affecting areas of their lives in ways that cannot be changed.

During my years of counseling women, I've found that we all share the same type of thinking at some point in our lives. We believe that we are unhappy in our marriages and then hurry toward the decision to leave before we get too old. We think that if we are only in our thirties, we can still attract someone else into our lives. Lori battled with the decision of leaving her husband because of the fear of raising a child by herself, but she knew that she was still young and hoped that maybe the next time she could attract the perfect man. This type of thinking makes us rush into divorces that we later regret.

Lori carries a lot of pain and has difficulty thinking that her life can change. The problem with her thinking is that she believes that she has to handle the pain by herself. She has tried many times to move forward and leave the past behind, but somehow the past keeps coming back to haunt and paralyze her. She was reminded that we don't have to handle the pain on our own. We can read hundreds of books and learn how to deal with our emotions, but it is much easier to allow the Holy Spirit to take the pain from us. We have to completely surrender our pain, our fears, our regrets, and our resentments and put them on the altar. It sounds too simple so we try to make it complicated. But the simplicity of God's love is amazing; it is by faith that we allow the healing to take place.

Satan will throw negative thoughts our way and remind us of our mistakes. However, we can choose what we entertain in our minds and negative thoughts don't have power over us unless we let them. We must remind Satan that we are forgiven because Jesus paid the price in Calvary. We must claim our mental healing. We will never find our purpose or fulfill our destiny if we continue to live in the past while feeling guilty and fearful about our future. We must move forward and allow God to work with us by changing our hearts and allowing us to be a light to others.

Clelia SantaCruz - LMSW

I understand the pain that Lori has endured, because I have dealt with the same issues. As a result, the words of Philippians 3: 13 have become real in my life: "Forgetting what is behind and straining toward what is ahead, I press on toward the goal to win the prize for which God has called me heavenward in Christ Jesus." We have to forget what is behind us! If we think about our past and our pain it should be to help others by giving our testimony, but not dwelling on it. God has forgiven us and forgotten our sins, so why should we continue to torture ourselves with regret?

"Real integrity is doing the right thing, knowing that nobody's going to know whether you did it or not."

-Oprah Winfrey

"Wisdom is knowing when to speak your mind and when to mind your speech."

-Unknown

Chapter 4

Our Powerful Words

I have found that the secret of success in marriage lies within the thoughts that we have toward it. Everything about us reflects our thinking; who we believe ourselves to be can impact not only our spouses, but our entire family, as well. If we don't like the way that our lives have turned out, we need to look at the choices we have made, the thoughts we have entertained, and the words we have spoken about our situation. Our minds are constantly racing, whether or not we are consciously directing them to positive or negative thoughts. When negative thoughts about our marriage enter our minds, we have the power to change them. If we spend most of our day dwelling on our troubles and talking to others about our circumstances, we are planting negative seeds and creating a situation where anger and resentment will destroy any chance that we have to turn our situation around.

When we constantly talk about our spouse and what he or she is doing or not doing, not only are we pouring negative energy into our marriage, but we are also attracting negative energy from the people with whom we communicate. We are unconsciously asking others to join with us in bringing additional misery into our lives. The words that come out of our mouths carry incredible power that will create what we are saying. The more we say something, the more we start to believe it in our hearts, and once it is in our hearts it will begin to affect our lives.

Mark 11: 23 tells us that if we tell a mountain to be removed and throw itself into the sea, and DO NOT DOUBT IN OUR HEARTS but BELIEVE what we SAY… then it will happen. That is powerful! We can speak to the circumstances in our lives that are causing us misery. Marital problems, financial difficulties, and disease have no power over us when we know our rights in Christ.

Thoughts of worry, fear, criticism, jealousy, and anger can produce sickness, depression, and misery in our lives. We can tell those thoughts to leave us and if we do not doubt in our hearts, they will leave. If we are filled with tension, fear, or anger we need to remember that tension exists in our minds first. Once tension is manifested in our mind, it will show up in our bodies and affect our hearts, blood pressure, and certainly our attitudes toward others. Negative emotions and the physical manifestations that go with them have roots in our minds and in our hearts.

All couples experience tension and conflict in their marriages. I know I do! It is what we do with the conflict that will decide the outcome of our relationships. We turn a conflict into an offense when we personalize what was said. Proverbs 20:3 says, "It is to a man's honor to avoid strife, but every fool is quick to quarrel." Many of us act like fools when we personalize what others say about us. We marry imperfect people like ourselves, and then expect perfection in our marriage. If we approach marriage with the commitment to understand, respect, and honor our partners, then times of conflict won't leave us feeling empty or negative toward our relationships. Differences of opinion are one of the main reasons that we argue with our partners, but we have to realize that they are different from us and that we don't have to agree on everything. Agreeing to disagree is one of the best things that we can do for each other. I am not saying that it is easy. There are times when I feel that my husband disagrees just to aggravate me, but that is probably not the case. I feel that way because everyone likes to live in a world where what we say to others is received and celebrated. When he disagrees with me, I can either take it personally or I can appreciate that he has his own thoughts and ideas. Most of the time, I think about making him disappear when he is being disagreeable, but that would not be a good thing. Effective communication involves listening, speaking and, understanding what the other person is trying to communicate to us.

When we make the decision to respect each other's opinions and we pray that God will give us wisdom and understanding, then the things that were said during a negative discussion will not have the same impact. But if we take personally what was said during a conflict, then we will be offended or insulted. Daily irritations, even when small, will cause accumulated anger that like steam will find a way out – sometimes explosively. When we experience one of those explosive moments, our words are full of fiery darts with the intention to hurt or humiliate the other person. I have been very good at throwing emotional darts at my significant other, but my relationship with Christ has brought me back to repentance.

Proverbs 19:11 states, "A man's wisdom gives him patience; it is to his glory to overlook an offense." Patiently dealing with conflict helps us to grow as people. When we have made a decision to practice love and follow Christ, but we continue to entertain negative feelings and speak negative words and we refuse to forgive, then nothing will work out for us. Making a decision to follow Christ is a commitment and it is not going to be easy. Many people who decide that they are going to "try this Christian thing," become disappointed because their lives are not instantly full of pure joy and happiness and then they consequently give up. Living a Christian life takes an incredible amount of commitment! We must follow God's word, which at times can be difficult because some of us have been operating by the world's principles and reacting to our flesh. When we make the commitment to follow Christ, we must live by God's principles and react to the Spirit. When we walk in the flesh and not in the Spirit, it seems that our enemy, Satan, leaves us alone; he has nothing to worry about because we will mess up on our own. The minute that we decide to follow Christ, not only do we get things thrown our way by our enemy, but God also puts us through school. He can't use us in His kingdom if we are not ready. We face many trials and tribulations so that we can be prepared to do His work. Pride, selfishness, and self-centeredness are fruits of the flesh and can keep us from experiencing the incredible blessings that God has in store for us. Believe me, I have personally suffered the consequences of having that rotten fruit in my life.

Many of us call ourselves Christians but live by the standards of this world, foolishly making the wrong choices. Being a Christian is being Christ-like and He certainly would not make the decisions that we make when faced with temptations. God knows our heart and when we pray that He change our desires, our hearts, and the circumstances of our lives, He will, but our motives have to be pure. Our prayer needs to be "change ME," because once we begin to change, we will see the circumstances of our lives with different eyes. The things that bothered us will no longer have power over us and the desires of our hearts will not be the same as before. One thing I can say for sure is that even in the midst of trials, He can give us incredible peace when we trust in His word.

Satan's mission is to destroy our families. Two of the weapons that he uses on a regular basis are resentment and unforgiveness. During counseling sessions many couples bring up issues that happened twenty years ago. They have been speaking negative words and continue to carry pain in their hearts that should have been released years ago. Many people don't realize that they are holding on to anger or resentment and that by not releasing it and continuing to be offended by their partner's comments or behaviors, they are allowing their enemy to steal their joy.

When we ask our Heavenly Father to give us wisdom during a difficult situation, He will bless us with understanding. The practice of understanding helps us to develop patience and character. God uses conflict to teach us to trust Him, to teach us to love like God loves us, and to teach us to forgive as He has forgiven us. We can experience the peace of God when during a conflict we respond without criticism and with a genuine desire to hear what our partner has to say. Most of the time, if I am mad at my husband, I will not want to hear what he has to say. However, allowing him to express his opinion and his emotions gives him validation for his feelings. If he feels validated, then the conversation goes on easily and we can both get our points across. If I operate in the flesh, I won't care about his feelings and we won't find a solution to our issue.

When we have a conflict, we must accept responsibility for the part that we have played in the conflict. We begin to grow when we take down the walls and our defensive attitudes and let God take our pain and give us the strength and wisdom to see things through His eyes. We should always ask ourselves if the argument is worth the emotional pain that we will endure as a result, because many times we argue about insignificant things.

God can make the impossible possible when we give our pain and release our situations to Him. I am not saying that every marriage can be saved by simply releasing our pain to God. There are many people who have been subjected to horrible abuse at the hands of their spouse. Advising someone who is in an abusive situation to just pray while they are being physically or sexually abused could place him or her in a dangerous situation. It can also cause this person to question God's involvement in his or her life. If you are experiencing that kind of abuse in your life, then you need to make the decision to get out of the abusive situation for your sake and the sake of those around you. What I am saying is that no matter what your situation is, God can give you peace in the midst of pain and disappointment if you allow Him to touch your heart. All you have to do is ask.

When couples come to my office for marital counseling, one of the first questions that I ask is if they see themselves growing old with their spouse by their side. Their response tells me what they are visualizing for their future and what kind of thoughts they are entertaining. If either of them cannot see their marriage lasting until tomorrow, then how can I help them? Consciously or subconsciously, they have made a decision about the outcome of their marriage and it will be difficult to change that decision unless they are willing to reconstruct their thoughts and their words. Proverbs 13: 2-3 states, "From the fruit of his lips a man enjoys good things....He who guards his lips guards his soul." And Proverbs 17: 27 says, "Even a fool is thought wise if he keeps silent, and discerning if he holds his tongue." The book of

Proverbs stresses the importance of our words. If you think and speak about divorce, then divorce will soon follow. Remember, nothing comes into existence unless we first think about it. Once we have that thought in our mind, we become impregnated with it and that thought will soon become a reality. When we are pregnant with negative thoughts, we will give birth to negative actions. Negative actions will give birth to sin and the Bible says that sin will give birth to death. I know that sin does not manifest in our lives unless we first entertain it in our minds.

    I recently saw a couple who came for counseling. The first words that came out of the wife's mouth were, "I don't want to be married anymore and I am going to file for divorce today." I was shocked as couples usually come to see me prior to making this decision. They might be thinking about it, but there is always hope that somehow their difficulties can be resolved. This woman knew exactly what she wanted and I knew that there was nothing that I could say to change her mind. She stated that they had been married for seven years and that for seven years she had been thinking about divorce. She looked at her husband and right in front of me said, "I don't love you, I am not attracted to you, and you bore me." I thought that she was cruel to say such a thing to another human being. We may think these things, but to say them, especially with such a harsh tone, is very painful to others. He looked at her and he smiled saying, "I know." I asked him how he felt after hearing her comments. He said that it hurt, but that he had heard it many times before. I tried to explain the power of words and how by entertaining thoughts of divorce and then speaking them aloud, she had manifested divorce. At this point she did not care. She had come to counseling because her husband had begged her to try one more time. She stated that she just wanted him to "get it" and to understand that she was completely sure that divorce would be the best thing for her. They had a young child, and the wife seemed to believe that her daughter would be happier if they divorced. I recognized the effects of Satan, because years earlier he had affected me in the same way, but there was nothing that I could do to help her. She was too far gone. I mentioned God and prayer, which actually offended her; she did not appreciate me bringing up spirituality.

Our Powerful Words

I continued to see her husband to help him transition. He was a smart and gentle man who loved his wife and was willing to do anything to save his marriage, but her heart was made of stone like mine had been in the past. I hoped that one day she might realize her loss. I prayed that God would touch her heart because she did not want to know anything about Him. According to her husband, she had had a bad experience being raised as a Catholic. I thought this was funny because again, it reminded me of myself.

If we want to have successful marriages, we must see our marriages as successful, no matter what is going on in our lives. We must speak positive words about our marriage and avoid associating with people who speak with pessimism and negativity about our circumstances.

You must use your imagination and create a positive image of how you want your marriage to be. Seeing the best in any situation, giving your spouse the benefit of the doubt, and allowing him or her to express his or her opinion without your judgment is something that you must strive to do in order to have a successful marriage. When you pray to God to allow you to see things His way, He answers that prayer and things begin to change in your life. God wants you to see the best in others, to see people through His eyes. Visualize the best qualities of your spouse, send a silent blessing, and say positive things about him or her. Instead of focusing on the negative, focus on the positive aspects of your relationship. If you don't have anything positive to say, begin to say what you would like to see in him or her. Say "thank you" to Jesus that your spouse is affectionate, kind, unselfish or any other trait that you would like to see change in his or her personality. Speak as if they are already what you want them to be; speak the answer not the problem. Believe that your circumstances will change by standing on the word of God.

Your worries and fears are due to your inability to align yourself with God's Word. God has not given you a spirit of fear, but one of love, and he has given you a sound mind, as well. He wants you to succeed in every area of your life and when you exercise your faith, circumstances in your life will begin to change.

Sometimes it is better to be happy than to be right. Your spouse might be doing wrong and you want to let him know that you are right and that he or she is wrong. But with God's help you can just let go and be happy rather than trying to make your point and be right. It is tough for me not to say what is on my mind and to not let my husband know that he is wrong. (Believe me, many times he is.) But the more I practice, the easier it becomes. I have argued with God many times, wanting Him to talk to my husband and to see his negative behavior. God's answer has always been the same. "Don't worry about him, you do what is right for you." But sometimes it seems right to hit him! I don't like that answer and I want my husband to be struck down by lightning! But God does not do it. When I finally let go, I am able to find peace. This is peace that I could have found sooner by doing the right thing. But no, it takes me a little while because I apparently want to feel those nasty emotions.

My peace of mind produces happiness in my life and I am learning to let go of things more quickly these days. Praise God that His mercy is fresh every morning and that when we desire to change, He gives us the strength to do it. As I continue to mature, I look back on my life and find that the things that I wish I could change have nothing to do with decisions about careers or finances, but mainly with the decisions that I made that impacted those who I love; the ways that I handled situations, the lack of patience that I showed to my children when they were young. Negative responses that I gave when someone wanted me to say something positive and actions that I took that impacted the lives of others – and maybe broke their hearts.

Today it is my desire to live my life, making the right decisions where my significant others are concerned. This way I can look at my life before I go to heaven and have peace, knowing that I expressed my love and my devotion to those who I loved.

Our Powerful Words

Everyday as I pass where my husband and children's pictures are displayed, I send them a blessing and say a positive statement about them (whatever quality I am trying to see in them at that particular time). I say it aloud if I am by myself, or silently if someone else is around. I see my husband and my marriage being a complete success, I see my children healthy, happy, and protected by angels. I see myself as God sees me, made in His image and therefore completely successful in every area of my life – spiritually, physically, emotionally, and financially. Practice visualizations and affirmations and you will see that those around you will start to change when you begin to see and affirm the best in them. I can tell you from experience that when I cease to visualize my spouse's positive qualities due to a conflict, I begin to concentrate on what I consider to be the negative aspects of his personality. Once I allow negative thoughts to enter my mind, it takes me longer to get back to the place that I need to be. The peace of God leaves me and I create unhappiness in my life and in the lives of those around me, until I realize that I am creating my own misery and I go back to visualizing the positive and affirming what God desires for me and my spouse, my situations, and my circumstances.

Our Powerful Words

"Trust in the Lord with all of your heart and lean not on your own understanding."

-Proverbs 3:5

"Because he loves me, says the Lord, I will rescue him: I will protect him for he acknowledges my name. He will call upon me and I will answer..."

-Psalm 91:14-15

Chapter 5

Releasing to God

2 Corinthians 4:18 tells us that, "You have to fix your eyes not on what is seen, but on what is unseen. For what is seen is temporary, but what is unseen is eternal." I believe that God can make a change when we allow Him to come to us in the midst of our trouble. When I tell him my problems and surrender them to Him, He gives me peace that surpasses understanding. Believe me, I pray about that daily because I have spent most of my life being self-centered and selfish, wanting my way at every opportunity. God has done major work in my life and put me through many trials. Some I have failed terribly, others I have begged to get out of – and he has said NO.

We won't get out of a bad situation unless we pass God's test. Some tests are harder than others and after all of these years of testing I have finally come to recognize the tests that God puts before me. Now I can say to myself, "OK, this is another test," and – after screaming and yelling – I see what the lesson is and I graduate from that particular course. I have lots of little passing certificates and many others with big red F's – especially from the course on PRIDE and PATIENCE. Those two lessons make me pull my hair out and I wish I could say that I have passed their tests. Not only do I have to take this class every time it's offered, but it usually comes with a lab and takes longer to complete. I am working on it and I believe that what has helped me the most is my desire to know Christ at a deeper level. I want to follow His commandments and have an intimate relationship with Him.

When I see my extended family, whom I do not get to see that often, they make comments about how much I have changed and how differently I behave. Being a rebel for so many years placed a label upon me that is difficult to erase. I know that I haven't made all of the necessary changes to be completely implemented by God, however, as we can see when we read His word, He uses all kinds of people. I can say with an honest heart that my true desire is to serve my Lord Jesus Christ and that everyday he changes me a little more.

I was reading my Bible one morning and wanted to understand a passage about releasing our faith. Surrendering all of our issues, pains, and disappointment to God is difficult. Most of us have, at some point or another, released our faith and given our issues to God. However, at times we take our problems back and entertain them in our mind once again with a desire to find a quicker solution. We think that God is too slow and that he might need our help. How foolish we are because then we have to start the process all over again. Nothing moves without faith. We must trust God with our issues and leave them on His altar. His timing is better than our timing.

I was reading from John 6:9 about the boy who had five small loaves of barely bread and two small fish. I asked Jesus to help me understand how the little boy's meal fed five thousand people. I asked Jesus why He didn't just feed these people by raining down food from heaven like He had done for Moses. I clearly heard Him say that we have to release to Him and He will provide for us.

In Old Testament time, God worked in different ways to show Himself to people and He even struck some when they disobeyed Him. We probably have it easier now – we just suffer the consequences for our mistakes instead of being killed on the spot. When we release something to God in faith, He will multiply our blessings. Everything starts with a seed!

Our Powerful Words

I imagine that little boy from John 6:9 was probably with his parents since he was only five years of age. His parents had probably already eaten their meal and were carrying the rest of it for their child. Can you imagine if Peter or John came to you and asked you to give up the only food that you had? Especially if you were far from home and there were no WalMarts around from which to buy food. I know what I would have said: "Are you kidding me? Sorry, but I am not giving my child's food away." But apparently that is not what they said. Either the parents or the boy gave their food to the disciples and the Lord blessed the food and fed five thousand men and their women and children. Wow, that is a lot of people! I can only imagine that the twelve baskets left over were given to the little boy's family and that they fed their entire family and friends for several days.

No one writes about the little boy's obedience or his release of faith. The book of John mentions him casually, but I truly believe there is a message in that passage not only about the miracle that Jesus performed, but also about the faith that one little boy and his family had and the blessing that they got in return. I felt that God was telling me how important it was to release everything in my life to Him. When I release what is in my hands, my heart, my mind, and even my bank account, He can release his emotional, spiritual, and financial blessing in my life. When I release my time and give it to Him and to others, He can bless me in other areas of my life. When I release my sickness, He can make whole again. I want God's blessings to govern my life. My security depends on Him, not whatever is going on around me.

I would be lying if I told you that worry doesn't enter my mind when things are not going the way that I think they should. When I realize that I am giving into negative thoughts, I begin to spend time in worship and then quickly find a tape, a book, or a Christian talk show that will lift me up. It has never failed that when I seek God I can find Him, He never leaves me; I leave Him by being busy and not spending time in His presence.

Clelia SantaCruz - LMSW

> "It's always too early to quit."
>
> -Norman Vincent Peale

> "The only people to get even with are those who have helped you."
>
> -Anonymous

Chapter 6

Letting Go of Resentment

When the significant others in our lives behave in ways that hurt our hearts or in ways we find unacceptable, instead of hurting them back – which is what our flesh tells us to do – we can choose to turn our troubles over to God. When we have unforgiveness in our hearts, it will affect every area of our lives. Our prayers will be hindered if we carry or harbor negative feelings toward our spouses, our parents, our children, or our friends. God cannot bless us when our hearts are full of resentment and unforgiveness.

I learned long ago that no one is important enough to interfere with my relationship with God.

We women have the tendency to remember things that happened twenty years ago. Our memories seem vivid in comparison to those of our male partners. Feelings that we experience in the present seem familiar to us because they are the same feelings that we have had in the past. They are painful memories of unfulfilled needs. When those familiar feelings come to the surface due to a comment made by our spouse or someone who we are emotionally involved with, we often respond with fury. We may be experiencing these negative emotions for not only the current incident, but for past incidents, as well. Why do we have such vivid memories of these incidences of pain from the past? Is it that we have masochistic tendencies and like to inflict pain on ourselves? Or do we like creating drama in our lives? Usually we experience these feelings because we never dealt with them when the original incident occurred. We must release it and put the past behind us where it belongs. If we surrender our pain to Jesus, He will heal our hearts! We might still have memories of a painful past, but it is up to us to keep the pain alive or to let it go.

Anger, resentment, hate, and unforgiveness will weaken our bodies. Statistics show that stress related disorders are the number one reason for doctor visits in America. A common cause found in stroke patients is stress caused by guilt, unforgiveness, fear, low self-esteem, and depression. This is a sad statistic, and in my years of counseling I have seen many people with fear, anger, resentment, and unforgiveness in their hearts. All of those feelings lead to stress, which can produce metabolism disorders, skin problems, high blood pressure, gastrointestinal problems, and even cancer. Stress also produces secretion of adrenaline, which can cause slow digestion, raise cholesterol levels, and make our hearts work more intensely. It is for this reason that Proverbs 22: 24-25 tells us not to make friends with a hot-tempered man, and to not associate with a person who is easily angered because we may adopt his ways and get ourselves ensnared.

When we respond with anger, it drives our spouse even further. The word tells us in James 1:20 that "anger does not bring about the righteous life that God desires." God wants us to practice self-control! I hear many of my clients say that they just can't help being angry because they have no control. Some say that their spouse drives them crazy to the point that they don't know what they are doing. I can definitely relate, but I know that we do have control and that the more we practice control, the easier it becomes. We have been programmed to react to any little thing that happens around us. Many of us learned anger by observation when we were children. We saw our parents respond to each other in ways that made us think that it was normal to immediately say whatever came to mind. Being assertive and not allowing people to run all over us is different than responding with anger. There are healthy ways of responding to or communicating with others, but it requires re-programming our mind daily by reading His word, communicating with God, and releasing the anger or the negative emotions that we are feeling. I found that the secret to releasing anger and resentment is to pray for the person who has offended me. I know that is probably the last thing that you want to do when someone has hurt you. But, doing so has helped me during times when I thought that I could not forgive a person who had treated me badly. When God tells us to pray for our enemies, and we do it because we are being obedient to His word, He will then bless us for doing the right thing.

Keeping track of our spouse's wrong doings is deadly to a marriage. What does God do with our sins? He forgives them. Why would we not do the same for others? Peter asked Jesus, "How many times should I forgive my brother when he sins against me? Up to seven times?" Jesus answered, "I tell you, not seven times, but seventy-seven times," (Matthew 18: 21, 22). When we reconcile with our mates it means that we are forgiving everything that they have done to us and we begin again with an open heart. If we want to work on our relationships with our significant others, we can probably start with something as simple as listening to what our partners have to say. Listening is the most important of all communication skills. We must know how to listen in order to make our relationships work. Listening tells our partners that we care about their feelings and want to work on whatever issue that they have brought up. Many of us neglect to listen by judging our partners the minute that they start to speak. If we listen to anything that they say, we just use this information to gather more evidence that we can use against them, or to form a stronger case to confront them with. Too often our purpose is to judge and to place blame.

Many of us like to read minds and we think that we know what our partners are thinking or are about to say. Mind reading is a definite way of blocking communication; we hear what we want to hear and disregard what our partners are trying to communicate to us. We concentrate more on body language than on what is actually being said. We guess their next sentence and begin to rehearse what our response will be. However, we can't listen if we are already thinking about the point that we will make the minute that we can get a word in. Being right becomes so important to us, that it prevents the relationship from growing.

The secret of living resentment-free is to be able to communicate any misunderstanding when it happens instead of letting it fester. In order to improve our communication skills, we must concentrate on listening and paraphrasing what our partners are telling us. We have all read how important it is to use "I" statements; we must state what we feel and leave out the blameful comments. When we are able to tell our partners what we hear as they speak to us, then we give them the opportunity to correct any misinterpretations in that moment. We are able to clarify and move on.

When we are angry, our partners will sense our anger even if we say nothing is wrong. Often times we are not able to express or define why we are angry; we just want them to see how angry we are. We must clearly define what we mean when we say that we are upset, angry, sad, or any other adjective that we use to describe our feelings toward our partners. If you say that you are upset, is it that you are worried or fearful? If you are fearful, state that you are upset because you are fearful and explain what you are fearful about.

I understand that sometimes we don't even know what the fear actually is. If you search deep in your heart, then you will be able to figure out why you are fearful. If it is because of jealousy, then think about why you are jealous. Is it because you don't want your spouse to think that someone is prettier, smarter, or thinner than you? Define what it is that you are fearful of and talk to your spouse about it. This way, it will be easier for your partner to understand why you are angry with him or her. Let him or her know the intensity of your feelings as well as how long you have been feeling that way and what caused you to be angry. You must avoid blaming your partner for the emotions that you are experiencing; if you do, your partner will become defensive and it will be difficult to state your point.

All human beings seek meaning in their lives; we strive to be understood, to be loved, and to be respected. When we lose intimacy in our marriages, we begin to pull back. Little by little we allow the enemy to fill our hearts with disappointment, negative thoughts about our partners, and negative thoughts about our future together. We soon find that we are not giving anything to them and that we are not receiving anything from them either. When we ask our partners for change, sometimes we ask them to change intangibles. We ask them to change things that are part of their personalities and are sometimes beyond their conscious control. They, in turn, feel threatened. When we ask that they be more loving and nice, or less critical and mean, then we must ask by being specific. If we feel that they lack respect, then we must ask for respect and explain what it means to us. It is the same when we ask them to be more loving; we must describe what "loving" means to us. Is it that we need to be told that we are beautiful more often; is it that we want more affection from them? We must be specific about what we ask for because no one can read our minds.

Some of us find this type of communication difficult because we don't know what we want. We know that we are missing something in our marriages, but we don't know what it is because we don't spend time deciphering our feelings. We just know that we are unhappy and we want an instant fix. However, sometimes we feel awkward asking for things that could make a positive impact in our relationships.

After many years, it has become clear to me that according to the law of reciprocity I will never receive from anyone what I am not able to give. If I want my husband to respect me, then I need to respect him in turn. If I want him to be more affectionate, then I must be affectionate toward him. My dog, Lola, is a perfect example of this concept. Lola is the sweetest, red-nose pit bull that anyone has ever met. Yet, people look at her and are immediately fearful due to the pit bull reputation. Once they get to know her, however, they express affection for her that Lola is eager to return. Lola will give us so much affection that we in turn have to caress and cuddle her. It is the same with our partners; we must give in order to receive.

Resentment can be released with prayer! What happens if we begin to pray as couples and allow God to heal our wounds, and heal our marriages? What happens if more husbands take authority over their families and become the spiritual leader of the home as God intends them to be? What happens if we women allow our husbands to take that role and we become submissive – knowing and trusting that our husbands love us like Jesus loves his church? Some of us don't even want the word submission to enter our vocabulary because it shows weakness and control by someone else. I know that those of you who know me personally are laughing right now and thinking "Clelia…you? Submissive?"

The word "submission" is not the problem! It is our misunderstanding of what submission is, not only for women, but also for men. I believe that women would not have a problem submitting to a husband who they know has the best intentions for them: A husband who loves them unconditionally, a husband who would never use his authority to manipulate. We can follow a husband who respects us and loves us, but not one who acts like a fool and shows his anger and his arrogance, expecting us to follow his command. That is crazy!

God tells us clearly the principles that we must follow in order for our marriages and anything else in our lives to work. The principles are the same for everyone and when we apply them, we can have success in our lives. God tells us that we must love, we must forgive, and we must give. He tells us to do unto others as we want done unto us. There are times when we think that we hear something inside us telling us to "Apologize," "Return that money," or "Be nice to that person." But we question the feeling and many times ignore it, not realizing that the Holy Spirit is trying to communicate to us. The more we ignore His voice, the less He will talk to us and the more desensitized we will become to His still small voice. God says that we will be blessed if we are obedient. He does not say that we will understand His message when we are obedient, but He definitely says that we will be rewarded. I want to be blessed and see the fruits of my obedience and therefore when I hear that small voice, whether I think it is me or the Holy Spirit, I follow it. We need to allow Him to open up the eyes of our spirit, and to allow us to see our situation the way that He sees it. If we don't allow God to help us to see the truth, then we will experience misery in our marriages; we tend to see what we want to see, and many times we only focus on the negative.

Our Powerful Words

Many divorces occur because our thoughts are not in line with the word of God, and because Satan can and will attack our marriages at every opportunity. If we do not follow Christ, we will be open for Satan's suggestions and we will fall for his temptations. Satan's mission is to destroy our families, and he has done a good job considering that statistics in this country state that 5 out of every 10 marriages will end up in divorce, with the average marriage lasting 9.8 years.

My ex-husband and I failed to nourish and nurture our relationship, and we ended up with a broken marriage. We allowed the enemy to take from us the most precious thing that God can give – a beautiful family. I am well aware that you might have negative feelings for your spouse that took years to develop. You might have needs that have not been met, or maybe you are experiencing pain due to infidelity, lies, deceit, and unfulfilled promises. All of these things lead to an incredible amount of resentment, which in turn creates unforgiveness, anger, and depression. If those feelings are not released to God, then they will affect you tremendously, making you miserable and taking your joy away.

Many times these layers of resentment will keep you from moving forward, but the only way to deal with a problem is to face it straight on. Deal with it and don't hide it under the rug because at some point it will show up again. If you ignore your issues, then any small conflict will become a much larger problem. The layers of resentment can get so deep that you feel like a volcano waiting to erupt. Resentment can bring incredible anger into your life, which affects you not only emotionally, but also physically. Remember that statistics show that most doctor visits are related to stress. Doctors have even linked resentment and anger to certain types of cancer. Resentment will keep you from seeing the good things that your marriage brings into your life. It will keep you from seeing the good qualities that your spouse has, the beauty of having a complete family, and the blessings that God gives if you practice love.

There are strong forces against us, but the forces that are for us are stronger and we must utilize them. It is much easier to give in to the temptation to end our marriages in hopes that our pain will end, than to fight for our family and for peace. We have the power to speak to the mountain and tell it to be removed from our lives, but we must have the faith that it takes to move a mountain. The only way that we can increase our faith is to spend time in the word of God daily, communicating with Him and being obedient to his Word.

Luke 10:19 tells us that God gives us power over Satan's power. In other words, the enemy has no choice – when we tell him to go he has to go! We can't just say, "Mr. Devil, please leave me alone! Pretty pleaassse?" NO! We have to use the authority given to us by Jesus. Speak with confidence! With Authority! If he sees fear, he will stay and drive you crazy! The Bible tells us that if we resist the enemy, then he will flee from us. Temptations for divorce can be cast down by reading what God says about divorce and what He says about us. We cannot change anyone but ourselves, though it is amazing how changes occur when we ask God to help us see things through His eyes and to soften our hearts to receive what He wants us to receive. When we lift up our spouses to Him, He begins to do work in them. We lift up our marriage, and He begins to heal the wounds. He removes the veil from our eyes so that we can find our piece in the puzzle and take responsibility for our actions.

When I work with couples, I have them practice different techniques that allow them to release their anger and their inability to forgive. I want them to become familiar with each other again in order to rebuild their friendship and intimacy. "Reciprocal reinforcement," is a technique that was established in 1969 by R.B. Stuart. It simply means that each person does something that his or her partner likes or enjoys. This gives couples the opportunity to work together for a common goal and it works to increase pleasure and commitment in the relationship. It is amazing how giving to others can make us feel; it is by giving that we receive. Both partners win by satisfying each other and making each other happy.

For example, I had a client who detested football, and when the season approached in September, she would begin to experience mood swings. She would dread Sundays because her husband, as she put it, "would be glued to the television set watching the stupid thing." This woman had already conditioned herself to feel negativity toward the sport, and her negativity grew worse every year. I instructed her to practice reciprocal reinforcement – to start looking at the game as a challenge, to begin noticing the rules of the game, and to maybe become acquainted with some of the players' names in order to open up her mind to a sport that can be quite fun.

Years ago I learned that if I wanted to spend time with my husband, I was going to have to learn to like football or I would be spending lots of time by myself. When my son, Josh, began to play sports at age five, I loved to watch him so much that it became easy to love the game and understand it. My son, Eddie, played soccer and I enjoyed watching him play, though it seemed like a very slow and boring game to me. I love football and basketball and my husband loves that I am able to enjoy the games with him. Our goal should be to try to enjoy each other's activities, whatever they might be, in order to create a bond that will successfully impact our marriages. By discovering activities that we both enjoy, we emphasize the strengths in our relationship and avoid resentment.

Clelia SantaCruz - LMSW

Our Powerful Words

"Do not ask the Lord to guide your footsteps if you are not willing to move your feet."

-Anonymous

"A happy person is not a person in a certain set of circumstances, but rather a person with a certain set of attitudes."

-Hugh Downs

Chapter 7

Flesh or Spirit

When circumstances in our lives make no sense and we fail to see the direction in which God is taking us, then we begin to wonder if we are out of His will. We have difficulty sensing His presence and we allow fear to enter our minds. His word tells us that He will never leave us or forsake us, but when we face negative circumstances, it is difficult to see that He is right there with us. When we make the decision to be led by our flesh and we fail to recognize His guidance, then we tend to make mistakes that cause regret and confusion. I know that I mess things up quickly when I make decisions based on my emotions. Galatians 5: 16 reads, "So I say, live by the Spirit, and you will not gratify the desires of the sinful nature." This tells us that if the Spirit leads us, then we will disagree with our sinful nature and we will have power over our flesh. When we don't have faith, we reject the Holy Spirit and become disobedient to the word of God. The flesh and the Spirit are in constant conflict, but we can win over that conflict when we choose to live by the Spirit.

When I counsel couples who are facing serious issues in their marriage, I find that the conflicts they experience stem from their desire to give into the flesh or give into their emotions. However, Paul tells us that if we keep on "biting" and "devouring" each other, we will be destroyed by each other (Galatians 5:15). Many people get married with the intention of finding completeness in another person and they fail to realize that when we have a void in our lives, we will have the same void after we get married. We confuse this void with a material lacking and we believe that someone else can help us feel better. We get married and think that our anxiety will go away, our depression will go away, and our need to be accepted will go away, but we are in for a rude awakening! No one can fill that void for us except Jesus Christ. Anytime that we are out of God's will, we will experience a void that is so difficult to understand. We feel as if we are missing something in our lives and we begin to fill the void with the wrong things. At this point, the enemy sees the opportunity to throw temptations our way and he puts thoughts in our minds that become real if we allow them to reside in us. If we would dismiss the thoughts quickly and get back to the word, then we would not face half of the obstacles that we face in our daily lives. No one can change us and we can't change anyone else, only our relationship with the Holy Spirit can give that complete fulfillment. It is difficult enough to begin a life with another imperfect human being, and it is especially difficult when we are expecting that other human being to fulfill our every need and give us validation.

Too often we make the mistake of rushing into situations because we have a need to belong. However, this need to belong will not be fulfilled by anyone except Christ. When our spouses do not meet our emotional needs, many of us begin to entertain the thought of leaving them; we experience the same emptiness that we thought would go away after marriage. At that point we need to stop, open our eyes, and see where we are individually failing in our relationships. Accepting responsibility for our actions is the first step to seeing the truth. We must remember that we feel the familiar emptiness when we are out of God's will, and it is not up to our significant others to make us feel whole.

Sometimes we make a mistake and the person who we are with is not the right person for us. When we do not walk with God, we will make all kinds of wrong choices. At these times we just need to forget our bad decisions and get on with our lives. When marriages end due to abuse or neglect, then it is acceptable; we don't need to be in a situation that is negative for us and for our children. But when marriages end due to boredom, selfishness, or plain insecurities, then divorce is not an acceptable choice. Love is a decision that we make everyday. At first, I did not see it that way, which is why I feel that it is important to write on this topic. When we feel that we are no longer in love and things look better on the other side, then we are being deceived. It has been said that when the grass looks greener on the other side, then we must try to water our own. If we take care of our own lawns, by watering and providing the necessary nutrients for them to grow, then our lawns will be just as green as our neighbor's. Relationships are like plants – we must nurture them, water them, and provide a good environment for them, and we will see them blossom.

God's number one commandment is that we love Him. The second is that we love others as we love ourselves. However, it is difficult to love those who have different opinions than our own. I realize that God has had so much to teach me about love through my marriage with Alex. Alex and I mirror each other, we have so much in common and it's wonderful when we agree. On the other hand, many of Alex's negative qualities are negative qualities that I see in myself, as well. God places people in our lives who will help us to grow, and I have come to the realization that God will not take me to the next spiritual level unless I begin to practice unconditional love for my husband. I have no problem showing unconditional love to my children. That is not a weakness for me; my children are special to me and I love them no matter what they do. When it comes to my husband, however, he better act the way that I want him to act and say the things that I want him to say, or I will be stingy with my love. But God has a different plan for my life; He has put me on this earth with someone who will challenge me in many areas. Everything that I am so quick to recognize as a flaw in Alex's personality is something that I need to work on in my own personality. We have both asked God to make a true change in our hearts; we want to live a life ruled by the Spirit and not by the flesh, to please God and not be ruled by our emotions.

Friends are a gift from God, and friendship is key to a successful marriage. I met a wonderful, godly couple that seemed to have it all together. They looked happy and acted as if they were best friends. When I asked them about their friendship, they replied, "We truly like each other and spend quality time together." Wow, what a concept! Spending time with a best friend who is also your spouse. I am able to understand that concept because my husband is my best friend. Alex and I spend a tremendous amount of time together, just enjoying each other's company.

Despite our friendship, we still have conflicts like everyone else, and at times it seems that we are not going to make it through the day. Our personalities are strong and it is difficult to accept that either one of us is wrong because we are both always right! We have had plenty of arguments about our children. It is extremely difficult for couples who have children from other marriages and expect their spouse's children to behave a certain way and to accept certain rules. No matter how mature and healthy a relationship is, children from prior marriages will bring unexpected conflicts, and we must be prepared to take these issues to God's altar and pray that He can talk to us and allow us to receive His word.

One day, I was upset at Alex for asking something about one of my sons in what I thought was a sarcastic way. At times, he feels that he can't say anything when it comes to my precious boys. He is right! They are precious in my eyes and no one can say anything unless they feel the same way I do. The problem with that attitude is that God gets a hold of me and quickly brings me to reality. That night, I was upset and went to bed early, not apologizing for my tone of voice or trying to understand what Alex was trying to communicate to me. He came into the room while I was half asleep and I woke up the minute that he got into bed. I clearly heard God say, "Apologize to him, tell him that you are sorry for arguing." I thought, "No way, I am not sorry, and why do I need to apologize to him? He needs to apologize to me for what he said." God repeated His command and I said, "No, I am not going to do it. I would like to hit him that is what I would like to do."

I immediately felt uneasy and knew that I could not get any rest that night unless I did what God was telling me to do. I got up, went to the kitchen, and got some cold water as if trying to swallow what God was telling me to do. I went back in the bedroom, feeling very uneasy and not wanting to be obedient. But I said "I am sorry about arguing with you today." The light was off and I was not able to see his face, but he said one word to me: "Ok." That one word made me mad again. I thought, "Ok, is that all you can say? You are a jerk!" I said to the Lord, "Look at him, he is not apologizing to me. He is the one that offended me!" I forgot that nobody can offend us unless we let them. I heard God say clearly, "Don't worry about him, you do what is right."

The peace of God came over me and I was able to feel at ease. I could have entertained negative thoughts about the whole incident and I could have lost my blessing, but I chose to follow what God told me to do. I chose to not care if I was wrong or if Alex was wrong (even though I knew he was). I want to hear from God and I have decided that I will do whatever He tells me to do. No matter what it is, I would rather do something because I think that He is talking to me, than to miss Him all together. But believe me it is not always easy!

When we spend time concentrating on our spouses' negative aspects, we will never be able to see the positive changes that God may be doing in them. We manifest the thoughts that we entertain in our minds. If we want to see them change, we must lift them up to God and pray about our situation, then we must begin to visualize the solution; we must imagine them displaying an attitude of love and acting in a way that aligns with the word of God.

I know how difficult it can be to see the best in someone when we are angry about the way that they are treating us and we believe that their behavior is wrong. When we are ruled by our emotions, it is impossible to see what God wants us to see. The Lord knows our heart and when we ask Him to change our desires, to convict us when we are not obedient to His word, and to show us the way, He does. I know that in my personal life, He convicts me of things that I have asked Him to help me change – words that I say or actions that I take. The minute that the words come out of my mouth, I am convicted and I am able to repent, but sometimes I don't care. I just want to say what is on my mind, and I do quite often. Then I suffer the resulting pain, which is my consequence for disappointing The Holy Spirit.

When we ask God to change our hearts, He changes our desires; the things that seemed appealing to us no longer have that affect. We begin to change and we desire to do things that please the Spirit and not the flesh. Then it is not the external things that make us happy, but the internal things of the Spirit. When we operate not with a self-centered attitude, but with an attitude from the Spirit, then what other people say about us won't hurt us. We can dismiss their comments and rejections because our validation comes from our Heavenly Father. When we take things personally, we will suffer every time because people have the tendency to hurt us. When we know who we are in Christ, then it is difficult to allow individuals to inflict pain in our hearts and we can quickly dismiss their comment.

I wish that I had known years ago what I know now, but it takes time spent in the word and in the willingness of God to follow His commandments. Divorce entered my mind and divorce manifested itself in my life. My family would still be together if I had allowed the Spirit of God to rule my life. In my first marriage, I spent entirely too much time concentrating on the negative aspects of my marriage and what I thought I was missing out of life. I was married at a very young age and felt that I was missing something. But I was not missing anything – I already had everything. I had a beautiful family, children who were healthy and well behaved, and a husband who loved me with all of his heart, but who at times did not show his love because he did not know how. He allowed temptations to over take him and his expressions of love became obscured. It was difficult to understand how a man who loved me so much could at times behave the way he did.

Today I am aware that we both made wrong choices and that every demon in hell was against us. I allowed Satan to win that battle because I saw what he wanted me to see. Eddie and I had issues like everyone else, but they were nothing that we could not have worked out. Temptation and sin entered our lives; he was doing things that did not align with the word of God and I began to find excuses for my sins. I

Our Powerful Words

felt that I was not receiving from him what I needed in my marriage, and soon I had the desire to find it somewhere else. I failed to realize that the only thing I was missing was a daily communion with my Heavenly Father.

When we spend quality time with our Heavenly Father, the voids in our life will be filled and complete. I did not know the importance of staying positive and was not aware that the words from my mouth were powerful enough to destroy or build my life. My marriage ended in divorce; one single bad decision impacted not only my life, but also the lives of my children, forever.

Holidays can be a stressful time for my sons; they have to divide their time between both parents. I love being around my boys and desire to spend any time available with them. However, they are grown men now and have their own lives, and their limited time is divided between their father and me. My grandchildren will have to divide their time between several households. Not only did my decision impact my boys, but it also will impact my grandchildren and their children.

Despite the effects that my divorce had on my family in the past, I have cancelled the curse of my divorce, in my generation and my children's generation, because I know that it can make a difference in their future. We need to know our rights to rectify the mistakes that we have made. My parents' marriage ended in divorce and that curse carried to me, and then I allowed it to affect my children – but NO more. I will not allow the curse to continue, because I am aware of my rights as a Christian and I have taught my sons that they must exercise their Christian rights, claiming the blessings and renouncing the curses.

Every Christian should learn to renounce his or her curses, because we pay for sins that were committed by past generations without even knowing it. We are getting closer to the end of time and Satan is increasing his attacks on marriage and families. The divorce rate in America has reached an alarming rate. We have made the decision that if something does not work we can discard it and cut it out of our lives.

Instead we should take responsibility for our actions and not make decisions based on impulse.

Successful marriages are rare, so when I find a couple who expresses love and affection to each other, I like to know the secret to their success. One of those couples is Jack and Martha Langham. I first met Martha when I joined a women's committee in our church. She showed strong leadership qualities that impressed me, and I decided to get to know her better. When I saw her and Jack together, I could see that they shared a special relationship. I saw them laugh and have fun. I mentioned to Martha that I was impressed when I saw them enjoy each other so much, because I knew that they had been married for many years. She responded that they truly enjoyed each other because they were best friends. That was a beautiful thing to say about her husband and we should all feel that our spouse is our best friend. She stated that they had been married for thirty-five years and I was thrilled to see the chemistry that they had with one another. I decided to ask them if they could share their experiences with me and tell me the secret to their successful marriage. I knew that the information they would give would be beneficial to this book.

Martha and Jack met at a very young age and started dating when Martha was thirteen and Jack was nineteen. They dated for about three years and got married right before Martha's last year in high school. Jack was anxious to start a family because most of his friends were married and had a family of their own. He had just completed his time with the United States Marine Corp and was ready to begin his life with the woman whom he loved. Martha got pregnant soon after their wedding, and she was forced to complete her senior year through correspondence. They left their home and moved to Yuma, Arizona. Martha felt that leaving her family behind was one of the hardest things that she would ever do, and later realized that it was probably the smartest move that they would ever make. It forced them to lean on one another for comfort and support and helped to shape their relationship.

Today Martha and Jack have two boys, Kevin and Timothy. They have attended the same church since they were born and as adults, they are both involved in some aspect of the ministry. Tim is an extremely gifted young man with an imagination from heaven. He is a full time staff member at Heartland Church with a variety of responsibilities. Kevin is a talented singer and he is always involved in helping those in need. Kevin's talents are more like his father's in that they both have an entrepreneurial spirit and like to work in the technical field. Kevin has become a successful businessman and is the president and co-owner of his company.

When I asked Jack and Martha the secret to their relationship success, they responded that their friendship and their communication skills have been key. What they remember the most from the beginning of their marriage is being so in love with each other that their time together seemed extremely special. Being away from their home and their families was hard, and they turned to each other for love and support. But, there were times when communication issues surfaced and at some point in their marriage they began to have issues with expressing their feelings. Jack would hold back his emotions and feelings and would not express them until they were overflowing. When his feelings came out, he could be very intimidating. Most of the time, they were aware of how much they could push each other. When they got to a snapping point, they would both withdraw until they had an opportunity to collect their thoughts and have a peaceful conversation.

Martha remembers feeling insecure at the beginning of her marriage because she was young and naïve about certain subjects. Jack took charge of most things and made most of the decisions that concerned the family. Years later, Martha attended college and little by little her personality began to change. The strength that she had always had started to surface, and her leadership qualities became a valuable asset in her career. Her insecurity turned into confidence and she knew that she and Jack's communication issues needed to be addressed. Martha had problems with Jack's tone of voice and his voice elevation. With her newfound confidence, she was able to communicate to him about the importance of staying calm and conversing in a way that was acceptable to both of them. Jack would do anything to please his wife, and made the necessary changes in order to have peace in his home.

When Martha began attending college, Jack showed interest in her career and was enthusiastic about every aspect of her experience. This made her feel valued and loved.

Many of us lose touch with our significant others when we go into a new field or begin a new career. Instead of supporting each other and becoming closer, we choose a new road that leads us further and further away from each other.

While I pursued my Master's degree, my ex-husband and I became strangers living in the same house. I was not able to share with him my experiences at school and my internships. One of my internships was at Child Protective Services. I witnessed disturbing things and I wanted to be able to come home and share them with him. But he could not listen to anything about children's abuse because it was too painful for him.

Jack allowed his wife to express her feelings and supported her in every possible way. The issues Jack had with communication continued to surface and he would often withhold his feelings. When they finally came out, it would be in an explosive manner. Jack grew up with a father who had difficulty expressing his feelings. Jack was not given positive affirmation as a child and therefore he grew up modeling his parent's behavior. Now he wishes that he could have better expressed his feelings to his children by letting them know how much he loved them, and by making them aware of their great qualities. He was always pleased with Kevin as he could relate to the technical skills that they shared. Tim, however, did not share those qualities. As a child, Tim had difficulty tying his shoes and it infuriated Jack. But Jack eventually realized that Tim's incredible artistic qualities are a gift from heaven, and today he is able to appreciate and be extremely proud of both of his sons.

Martha remembers feeling beaten down about Jack's inability to express his feelings; she felt as if all of their problems were coming at her at once. Conflict management and expression of feelings were skills that she wanted to master. With the help and education that she received at school, she was able to learn skills and techniques that would help her not only in her marriage, but also at work. She let Jack know that his behavior was not going to be tolerated and that he needed to find healthier ways of expressing his feelings. Jack learned that if his voice got too loud, the conversation was over. During heated conversations, Martha began to realize that they were talking about two different things. She would stop the conversation and say, "Let's start over because I don't think we are on the same page." Once the conversation started over, they would discover that one or both of them had misinterpreted something that the other had said, and that that's how the conversation got off track.

One of the most important aspects of Martha and Jack's marriage is their love for God. They have attended church for their "whole lives." Their true desire is to please their Heavenly Father and keep the covenant that they established with Him and with each other. Martha and Jack have not allowed the thought of divorce to enter their minds. As I have mentioned throughout this book, the thoughts that we entertain in our minds will manifest in our lives.

After years of marriage, Martha and Jack attended a program called "Pathways," where they both discovered who they were and how God saw them. This helped both of them appreciate their partner's uniqueness and talents. It also opened Jack's heart on an emotional level that he had never experienced before and it softened his spirit toward his wife.

Another important aspect of their marriage is their awareness of the difference between sex and intimacy. Martha remembers reading a magazine and finding in it exactly what she wanted to tell Jack but could not say it. She gave him the magazine and told him to read an article that stressed the importance of touch and affection without sexual activity. Many women have shared similar problems with intimacy during our counseling sessions. They feel that their husbands cannot show affection without desiring sexual pleasure. These are two separate things and it is extremely important that we distinguish between them. Early in their marriage, Martha and Jack learned how to express nonsexual affection and intimacy and it brought them closer to each other. Their friendship continues to be a major part of their success. They knew how important it was to experience intimacy with each other and they took time to get away at every possible opportunity without the children in order to focus on each other. Friday night was date night and they would leave the children in good hands while they went out to enjoy each other's company.

One of Martha and Jack's close friends admitted to them that she was jealous of their special relationship and the fact that they would often take vacations by themselves. At times they did not have enough money to travel, but getting away to have quality time is a priority in their lives. Their friend has the money to go away anytime that she wants to, but chooses only to do so when she can involve business with pleasure. It is fine to get pleasure out of business trips, but when we can take the time to go on a trip just to be together, it sends a great message to one another that says, "You are important to me." Having a successful marriage takes work, commitment, and love; when we begin to take each other for granted, we will suffer the consequences.

Our Powerful Words

"Death is not the greatest loss in life. The greatest loss is what dies within us while we live."

-Norman Cousins

"No person was ever honored for what he received. Honor has been the reward for what he gave."

-Calvin Coolidge

Chapter 8

The Laws of the Universe

Universal laws or principles that we can learn and apply in our lives can be found in a book that is full of wisdom and promises from above – the Bible. God, the creator of the universe, established principles and laws that, like the law of gravity, can't be broken. God tells us not to worry about our lives, what we will eat or drink, or about our bodies. I know that all of us, at one point or another, have worried about our situation. Many people make a habit of worrying about every little thing in their lives.

I have seen clients who worry that things are going to turn out badly in their lives. They believe that if they think this way, then they won't be disappointed if something bad does happen. What kind of nonsense is that? Thinking negative thoughts so that I won't be disappointed when the negative things come to pass is not only nonsense – it is ridiculous! That type of thinking will take you nowhere. People who think that way will encounter misery in their lives because they will attract what they are expecting. Our words and our vision determine the kind of life we will have.

Matthew 6 teaches us one of God's principles that must be followed in order to have success. Verse 33 tells us that we should first seek the kingdom and His righteousness, and that things will be given unto us. What things? Jesus specifies all of our needs in chapter 6:25.

When He talks about seeking His kingdom, He is talking about following His principles and operating under His laws. Faith and love are principles that we must follow. To love the Lord with all of our hearts is the number one commandment or principle and the second is to love our neighbor as ourselves. Loving our neighbors is difficult, but it is one of the greatest commandments and we must obey it if we want to reap the benefit of following God's principles. If we haven't been showing love to our neighbor, then we must begin doing so. We can't do it on our own; we must first ask God to change our hearts and to change our selfish desires.

If we continue to be self-centered instead of God centered, then we will never be able to practice love with those around us. In Luke 17: 21, He says that the kingdom of God is within us. If the kingdom of God is within us and He tells us that we must seek the kingdom, then the answer is already within us. All that we need to live a successful life is inside of us, but we still have to be aware of it and take action.

Another principle revealed to us by God has to do with faith. In Luke 17: 5-6 the apostles ask Jesus to increase their faith. His response is that if they have faith as small as a mustard seed, then they can say to the mulberry tree to be uprooted and planted in the sea and that mulberry tree will obey them. Jesus gave all of us the same measure of faith and it is up to us to exercise it. The more that we exercise our faith, the more that it will increase! These laws operate the same way as the law of gravity. We know that if we throw ourselves from the top of a building, then we are going to splatter our brains all over the pavement. There is no doubt about that one.

The law of sowing and reaping is another law that we can count on to work as it was intended. God's laws bring results into our lives because our Heavenly Father created them that way. But we also need to pay attention to the motives for which we do things, as our intentions will determine what we get in return. If we give out of our desire to be seen by others, or for any other reason that goes against the pure thoughts of God, then we won't receive the WHOLE reward. When we don't get what we expected, we quickly determine that the law does not work, but we fail to realize that we left some things out. I can't say that the principles of God only work when we have a pure heart, because I have seen non-Christians use them and reap their benefits. What I can say is that God tells us that we will reap benefits and have no sorrow when we act with a pure heart.

People of the world refer to these principles as a science that can be learned by anyone. Non-believers as well as believers have used these principles to their advantage. The distinction is that when we believers in Christ live by these principles, we are claiming our inheritance from God and we are giving Him the glory. When we have a personal relationship with Jesus Christ and receive the gift of the Holy Spirit, our lives are not only transformed in every area, but we can also be completely successful and have no voids in our hearts and no sorrow. Non-believers who apply the laws of the universe might be able to attract great things into their lives by having the right thoughts, saying the right words, and having the right attitude. But they will continue to experience problems in other areas of their lives because money, fame, or a good marriage can't take the place of the Holy Spirit. No amount of money in this world can buy health, true friendships, love, peace, or any of the blessings that we receive from our Heavenly Father.

Money without Christ gives us more opportunity for sin; when we have a void, we will fill that void with drugs, alcohol, or anything else that will give us a rush or fill our lives momentarily. Money makes it easy for us to obtain things that can numb us for a while. Worshiping anything other than God produces sin in our life and sin produces death. Romans 6:6 says, "The mind of the sinful man is death, but the mind controlled by the Spirit is life and peace." Christians have eternal life through Jesus Christ our Lord and savior and the peace that He gives us is priceless. We must know God's laws and be able to receive the truth that He has given us in His word. We cannot receive the truth of God unless we are ready, and I hope that you are at that place in your life.

God gave us a gift when He sent his only son to die for us and I know that as Christians we understand the gift we received – but do we know what to do with it? Don't put your gift up on a shelf and forget to use it, because you will miss all the blessings that can make you successful in every area of your life. Claim your inheritance so you won't continue living life defeated, poor, broken, sick, angry, and depressed. We have to realize that God cannot come down from heaven and fix things for us. We must realize that He has already done everything that He can do and it is up to us to do the rest.

The kingdom of God is within us and Jesus tells us to seek it. When we apply our faith and let our actions follow, then the mountains of our lives will begin to move. I imagine that God rejoices when we get it. He intended for us to have success in every area of our lives – spiritual, physical, emotional, and financial. It is our own inability to align ourselves with His word that keeps us from experiencing His glory. God can't give us a blessing greater than what we believe we can get. Mathew 9:29 says, "according to your faith be it unto you." In other words, it is up to us to receive the blessings that He has in store for each one of us. It is a matter of obedience, as all of God's gifts are available to us the minute that we choose to obey. We must have love for and faith in the Lord in order for His truth to be revealed. When we allow our hearts to experience God's love, then we will see His blessings. Our faith will make it happen!

Our Powerful Words

"Talk happiness; talk faith; talk health. Say you are well, and all is well with you, and God shall hear your words and make them true."

-Ella Wheeler-Wilcox

"What if you gave someone a gift, and they neglected to thank you for it—Would you be likely to give them another? Life is the same way. In order to attract more of the blessings that life has to offer, you must truly appreciate what you already have."

-Ralph Marston

Chapter 9

Planting Good Seeds

I have always loved a story that I once read about a family that was moving into a new town from a different State. They had their belongings with them and stopped at the first gas station that they saw to fill up. The attendant was outside and they asked him "What kind of people live in this town?" The attendant responded with another question! He asked them "What are people from your old city like?" They stated that the people from the city they were coming from were rude and obnoxious. The attendant responded that they were going to find the same kind of people in their new town. At the same time, another couple pulled up and they also had just moved into the town. They asked the same question to the attendant that the other couple had asked. The attendant responded with the same question that he had asked the first family. "What are the people from your old city like?" The couple responded that they were wonderful and friendly and that they would miss them very much. The attendant then said that they would find the same kind of people in the new town. The first couple, upon hearing his answer became upset and told him that he was lying because he had told them differently. The attendant said, "You will find that people are how you expect them to be."

When we expect others to be selfish and rude, we will usually receive what we expect from them. Our attitude toward our circumstances will determine the quality of our lives and relationships. What we have in our hearts is what we will attract. One of my relatives constantly gets taken advantage of by others. If she buys an item, the item is usually defective and she has to return it. If she calls a repairman, he will usually do a bad job and she will have to call someone else to fix it. She will tell you prior to their arrival that whoever comes is going to do a horrible job because "people just don't care these days." I have tried to explain to her many times that she attracts bad service because she expects it. She argues and says that it happens even when she is not expecting it. Her vocabulary is extremely negative and it does not matter what I say, she continues to make negative comments about most things in her life. I have prayed that God will place someone in her path who will help her grow because I am obviously too close to her and not able to impact her.

Our personal relationships work in the same way. When we think about our marriages, the image we visualize should be one in which we are having fun and loving each other. We must see ourselves being best friends, laughing, and having great communication. We need to visualize our children as happy and healthy. If you are not able to see these things in your life, you must practice until they become a reality in your heart. Remember the times when you and your spouse were happy, maybe at the beginning of your marriage. Remember when your children were not out of control, maybe a time when they were young and you could still reach them. See your children being productive, loving individuals who want to serve God.

Sometimes we need to physically see things in order to visualize them better. Obtain a picture of your husband or children at a time where everything was wonderful and keep that picture around at your office, in your bedroom, or in any other place where you spend time. Concentrate on positive feelings and soon you will think differently about your situation. Once your attitude is changed, the manifestation will follow. You will have faith to move that mountain out of your life.

Our Powerful Words

Learn to identify your negative thinking patterns and destroy them at their roots by replacing them with positive thoughts before they begin to produce fruit. When a negative thought enters your mind, replace it with something positive. The more that you entertain positive thoughts, even if you have not received your answer, the easier it will become for you to imagine the changes with your heart and with your mind.

God's laws and the principles are real and according to the law of sowing and reaping, we must realize that actions have consequences. When we expect the worse from others, it makes us act negatively toward them. I have decided to do to others what I want done to me!

I first heard of the law of reciprocity from one of my brothers when he was about fourteen and I was eleven or twelve years old. He would talk about that law as if he had been practicing it for many years. I could barely pronounce it, much less know what it meant, but he told me that whatever we did was going to come back to us. I always hoped that the abuse that he put me through as a child would come right back to him. I am sure it did in some way or another. Today, he and I are very close and communicate regularly. I never forgot that law and have used it in my life ever since I was a child.

Everything we do has a way of coming back to us. I have always known that my actions would carry consequences. The consequences don't always come in the same package, but in ways we don't even realize. Our motives need to be pure; if we want something positive to come our way, then we have to plant positive seeds. Negative seeds will produce a negative crop. We can't give of ourselves due to our need to be accepted or loved. We must do it because we have a true desire to help others and are being obedient to the word of God.

Jesus tells us to love one another, not because of what we will get in return, but because as James says, it is "the royal law" (James 2: 8). When we practice the law of love, we can experience what Corinthians 13: 4 says about love. "Love is patient, love is kind. It does not envy, it does not boast, it is not proud. It is not rude, it is not self-seeking, it is not easily angered, it keeps no record of wrongs. Love does not delight in evil, but rejoices with the truth. It always protects, always trusts, always hopes, and always perseveres."

Our Powerful Words

> "The future belongs to those who believe
> In the beauty of their dreams."
>
> -Eleanor Roosevelt

> "Every time we open our mouths, men look into our minds."
>
> -Anonymous

Chapter 10

The Law of Attraction

Clients come to my office and ask me why they repeat patterns of behaviors that they no longer want to repeat. They want to know why they continue to attract the same kind of people who bring unhappiness and disappointment into their lives. My answer to them is that all of us have a certain kind of energy or signal that we give out according to what is in our hearts. The beliefs that we have about ourselves are projected to others and they will bring to us what we are unconsciously seeking. If you like to take care of others to make yourself feel accepted and loved, then you will attract people who can take advantage of you. If you are untrustworthy and deceitful, then you will attract someone who will unconsciously accept those traits because he or she might have them within themself. If you cannot understand why you keep attracting the same kind of individual into your life, then you need to look at yourself. You need to figure out how you can change those traits in your personality in order to attract a different kind of person into your life.

If you have controlling issues within you that you have not resolved, then you may attract controlling people. Some people tell me that they don't understand how they attracted an abusive husband because they have never been abusive toward anyone. But if they grew up in an abusive home, then that is what is familiar to them. Statistics show that people who lived in an abusive home tend to be abusers or attract abusers, because those traits are passed down from generation to generation.

We can also attract people who possess traits that we don't have in order to internalize their trait. A person who has difficulty relating to others is usually attracted to someone who is popular and never met a stranger. A person with an inability to make decisions might be attracted to someone who is decisive and strong. Many times this law of attraction can be a positive thing, and other times it can create problems if we begin to lose whom we are in order to keep the relationship. When we depend on another person for traits that we would like to have or develop, we lose control and are no longer in charge. If we stay in a relationship because we don't know how to make friends but our significant other does, then it creates a dependency on that person and at some point resentment will develop.

There are times, however, when dependency on each other can be a healthy thing as it can bring balance into our relationship. Let's say, for example, that I am not organized even though I would love to be. I have tried to be and have wasted time because it does not come naturally. I could always pay someone to do it and concentrate on my strengths, or I can allow my significant other to help me in that area. I can also help him in areas that are his weaknesses. We give to each other and thereby create balance.

We can learn the most from examining relationships that are highly charged emotionally, because they show us the parts of us that we need to either accept or change. One of my clients, Karla, married an alcoholic. As a child, she grew up with a mother who was addicted to alcohol. Her mother was an abusive woman, neglecting Karla and her siblings on a daily basis. Growing up was a bad experience; instead of enjoying her childhood, Karla became the adult in that family. She had to grow up fast and be the caretaker for her mother and sisters. Her mother would begin to drink early in the morning and when Karla was an infant, during the early attachment phase, she failed to give Karla the love and security that she needed. As an adult, Karla failed to develop healthy coping strategies, and she had issues with self-esteem, boundaries, and communication.

Years later, when Karla met her husband, Roy, she never thought that she was going to repeat her childhood. Roy was an alcoholic and an abuser just like her mother had been when she was a child. Karla came to my office wanting to find answers as to why she had married someone with the same issues as her deceased mother. She wanted to know how to break free from the abuse that she had endured with an alcoholic mother and was presently enduring with an alcoholic husband. Lastly, Karla wanted to know how to make better decisions.

Many people forget that as adults, we have options that are not available for us as children. We can't choose our mothers or fathers, but we can certainly choose the kinds of friends or significant others who are in our lives. We don't have to put up with people who hurt us and abuse us. God says to love one another, but He does not say that we need to be in situations that are negative for us. Proverbs 12:26 talks about a righteous man being cautious in friendships; if we are not cautious with the people who we surround ourselves with, then the wicked will lead us astray. Karla did not choose the right friendship. There were signs available for her during the attraction phase, but she chose to look the other way.

Karla never learned to express her feelings; in order to protect herself from her mother's abuse, she was forced to restrain herself from stating her opinion or expressing her pain. Karla became numb and restricted important parts of her personality in order to keep her mother from lashing out at her. Those parts of her personality that were restricted as a child continue to be restricted as an adult. Now she must break free of those restraints by learning to communicate her feelings and by establishing healthy boundaries. Instead of boundaries, Karla had created walls. Walls are unhealthy coping mechanisms that keep us from knowing ourselves and knowing others. They prevent us from experiencing trust, closeness, and the gifts that others can give to us.

Karla was attracted to Roy because he was familiar to her. She was not aware of what attracted her to him, but the more time that she spent with him, the more comfortable she felt in his presence. By the time that she noticed how similar he was to her mother, the relationship had already developed and, according to Karla, she was no longer able to end it. You can always end a relationship that is abusive. My client does not know how to get out of situations that are harmful to her and until she learns to protect herself, she will continue to be in abusive situations.

Through objective judgment, Karla now knows that her relationship is negative and is aware that Roy is doing nothing to make personal changes in his life, but she is not taking any steps to end the abuse. She fears being without him and the thought of ending the relationship brings her physical and emotional distress. Karla and Roy have a symbiotic relationship, where she gives due to her desire to belong and be needed and he receives due to his own selfishness.

A series of studies has been done about the importance of an infant's need to feel attached to his or her caregiver. The response that we get from our mother will have a great impact on our ability to form relationships. If our needs are not met, we will become fearful, have difficulty making decisions, and, as adults, only feel complete when in a relationship. Even when the relationship brings us more grief than joy, we make reasons for staying that don't make sense to anyone else.

Karla's need to be in a relationship overrules her judgment and controls her actions. She is over-ruled by her emotions because she is used to regressing to her old patterns of behavior and negative thinking. Karla seems to spend an enormous amount of time worrying and being fearful about her life and her decisions. But fear corrodes our soul and keeps us from thinking clearly. I stressed to her the importance of keeping calm, because tension will block the flow of positive thoughts. We can't think positive thoughts when we are worrying about things that we have no control over. If our minds are relaxed, then a solution to our problems can emerge, especially if we allow The Holy Spirit to give us wisdom.

Our Powerful Words

We can't have a new life when we have the same old thinking. God wants to take us to new levels, but we must change our limited thinking by renewing our mind and releasing negative thoughts. Replacing our negative thoughts with the positive word of God is necessary if we want to grow and experience the gifts of the Spirit. I would never tell a client to divorce her husband unless I believe that she is being abused. Karla's husband was abusing her on a daily basis, and she is better off praying for him than staying with him and enabling him to continue with his pattern of abuse. Only God can make a change in Roy and she does not need to stay in an abusive situation. I am not advising divorce, but I am advising that she set boundaries and not allow abuse in her life.

I have heard people question God's involvement in their lives when their husband or child has chosen to reject Christ and live in sin. All I can say is that the word of God is very explicit in what He will and will not do. Peter 3:9 tells us that He does not want anyone to perish and that He waits patiently for us to come to repentance. He will not force Himself on anyone. It is our choice to come to Him. As spouses and parents, the only thing that we can do for our loved ones is to pray that God will open their spiritual eyes and remove bad influences from their lives. We must pray that He places the right people in their path and that the angels of heaven watch over them daily. I pray that prayer for my brothers and relatives who are not living their lives for Christ. I am confident that I will see every one of them in heaven when I reach that part of my journey. Our prayers release the power of God into their lives and we must continue to intercede on their behalf.

Philippians 4:8 tells us that, "Whatsoever things are true, whatsoever things are honest, whatsoever things are just, whatsoever things are pure, whatsoever things are lovely, whatsoever things are of good report; if there be any virtue, and if there be any praise, think on these things." The law of attraction indicates that we will attract what we believe in our heart. The thoughts that we entertain in our minds create a certain kind of energy that brings back to us what we give out. When we begin to entertain thoughts of divorce and concentrate solely on our anger, our disappointments, and the negative traits of our spouse's personality, then our marriage won't have a chance. If divorce is what we entertain in our minds, then divorce is what will manifest in our lives.

"Life is ten percent what happens to you and ninety percent how you respond to it."

-Lou Holtz

"Half an hour's meditation each day is essential, except when you are busy. Then a full hour is needed."

-St. Francis de Sales

Chapter 11

Visualizing Intimacy in Your Marriage

I can't tell you how many couples that I have seen since I started counseling where the number one problem is lack of sexual desire on the wife's part. A common issue between my clients is that the husband usually wants more sexual involvement from his wife. Some individuals want sex every day and some would prefer to have it several times per day. I find it difficult to believe that anyone can experience passion, romance, or intimacy if sexual intercourse is performed several times per day; it seems to me that it would become mechanical to have that many sexual encounters – unless you are newlywed! For most women, sexual appetite decreases after several years of marriage. But if you are one of those women who continue to be just as passionate as you were when you first got married…may God continue to bless you!

Sexual intimacy is only a problem when one spouse does not enjoy the frequency of which she or he is asked to perform a sexual act.

The Bible gets brought up a lot during these counseling sessions and it amazes me how certain parts get taken out of context. I recently met with a couple where the husband quoted 1 Corinthians 7:4. This verse says that the wife's body does not belong to her alone, but to her husband, as well. My client stated that his wife was not fulfilling her marital duty to him and therefore he "should just take [her body]," because it was his according to the Bible. She considered this rape and I had to agree that a forceful sexual encounter is, in fact, rape. My answer was not well received by her husband. He became very upset at this accusation. I asked if he had read the rest of the Bible – particularly 1Corinthians 13: 4 where he is instructed to place his wife's needs above his own. He had not read that chapter (or had not paid attention to it). This client is not the only one who has mentioned 1 Corinthians and it saddens me to hear about couples who experience issues related to sex.

Sexual problems are a big issue because they affect every other area of marriage. Many times women are just exhausted at the end of the day. Men fail to realize that women get tired and run out of energy when they are taking care of children's needs, especially if they are working full time. I could see the frustration on one client's face when her husband had no understanding of what she went through during the day as the mother of a two-year-old and a nine-month-old.

In my past relationship I found myself experiencing the same problems that some of my clients were talking to me about. I did not know the power of meditation back then. But as soon as I discovered meditation and made it part of my daily life, I learned that I can change any area of my life by spending time thinking about what I want instead of what I don't want. After all, people who fantasize about sex throughout the day are going to be more sexual than those who don't.

I asked one of my clients how often he engaged in sexual fantasy and he responded "all day." I wonder how some men get any work done! I explained to him that by thinking about it all day, he desires sex more and more. My prescription was for him to fantasize less, but for his wife to begin to fantasize on a daily basis. I explained to her how it works and she looked at me as if I were crazy. I promise you – I am not!

As I have mentioned throughout this book, you will attract whatever you concentrate on, meditate on, or entertain in your mind. I believe that if people engage in sexual fantasy about their partners, then they will be more sexually attracted to them. I know that people don't want to think about things that they don't want to do. But instead of thinking that sex is another chore, begin to think that you are having a great time, enjoying every minute of it, and receiving the great pleasure that you deserve. Sex should not be something that you dread, but something that you enjoy.

Women need to enjoy sex as much as their husbands. When they don't, they are missing out on a wonderful experience that is not only good for our marriages, but good for us – physically and mentally – as well. Statistics show that women who enjoy sex are healthier and happier than those who don't. Besides, it burns a lot of calories and is a great way to lose weight! Many husbands tell me that prior to getting married, their wives were just as sexual as they were. During the attraction phase, we want everything that the other person wants. Therefore, women are not lying when they say that they love sports or act as if they enjoy sex as much as their partner. I believe that after being married for a while and getting comfortable in their new environment, reality hits home and people realize that they actually don't enjoy certain activities as much as they did during the attraction phase. During that phase, they would have hung upside down from a tree just to please or be with that particular person.

A lot of people are romance addicts and don't even know it. The drama of a new relationship makes them enjoy whatever activity they do with their partner until one day, the romance phase begins to die, the connection that they once felt ceases to exist, and problems begin to arise. Watching football on Sunday afternoon is no longer enjoyable and sexual encounters don't have the same flavor. We are in trouble when that happens, but it happens because we never connected at a deeper level.

If we don't have a friendship with the person who we married, then we are missing the greatest piece of the puzzle. Friendship is the foundation of our relationships. If at the beginning of our relationship we deceive the other person by acting as if we enjoy all of the things that he or she enjoys, then we create a relationship based on deception and at some point we will be found out. If we allow the chemistry that we feel for that particular person to blind how we truly feel about certain things, then once the attraction phase is gone, all of those things that we did to please him or her will begin to annoy us tremendously. However, attraction based on mutual likes will develop into something real that we both can enjoy and it will bring to us a long lasting relationship.

Many books have been written about the power of the mind and the fact that our subconscious can't distinguish between reality and fantasy. If you don't believe it, look at the way we react to movies. We know that they are not real, but we can get so emotional that it makes us cry or experience fear. It is the same when we begin to visualize, fantasize, meditate, or create a mental picture in our mind--the more that we do it, the more that we will attract what we are thinking about. If you begin to see yourself – in detail – enjoying every aspect of your marriage, particularly the sexual intimacy between you and your spouse, then you will begin to experience the emotions as if they were actually happening. This does not happen overnight, but I promise you it will happen and you will be able to see the changes in your relationship. We all like to feel loved and desired and when women are afraid to give a compliment to their husbands because it could turn into a sexual encounter, then we are sending them a negative signal. When our husbands go to work and other women send them positive signals, they will receive them and possibly make wrong choices that could have been avoided it if we were making them feel wanted and special at home.

I am going to guide you through a visualization exercise where you can see yourself enjoying making love to your husband. Please don't allow negative thoughts such as, "This is a Christian book…I can't believe she is describing a sexual encounter." God created sex for our enjoyment. The Bible tells us that we should not deprive each other sexually. According to the apostle Paul, we should only deprive each other by mutual consent and only for a time so that we can pray. Boy, it sounds to me like our time should be spent making love and praying, I wonder when we do any work! Seriously, this exercise will help you develop desire for you husband that will be incredibly beneficial to your marriage. Practice it daily as much as you can. Remember that you will attract what you entertain in your mind.

Our Powerful Words

1. Sit in a comfortable position in a chair or lie down on your bed. Close your eyes and take ten deep breaths. Imagine that you are in a beautiful place with lots of color and soft cushions. Make this place be somewhere that you would love to be any time you feel like getting away.

2. You can hear your favorite romantic song playing and no one is around. You are all by yourself. The temperature in the room is perfect and the aroma of your favorite candle is in the air.

3. You are feeling beautiful and sexy. Your body is perfect; every part of you is beautiful no matter your weight or what physical flaws you may think that you have. You like yourself! You like who you are physically and mentally, and there is no stress in your life. No money issues, no children around, no in-laws, no job related problems. Everything is perfect in your world.

4. You see your spouse walk in and he looks extremely attractive. You feel the attraction that you felt when you first fell in love with him. You look at him and you appreciate every part of him. You feel incredible closeness. You feel a connection with him that you have not experienced before… He walks toward you and brings you your favorite gift. It could be roses, it could be chocolates, it could be a beautiful piece of jewelry, or whatever makes you smile. You look into his eyes and you see love…you feel the same about him.

5. He gets closer to you and begins to touch your face in a very gentle way. He then begins to kiss you the way that you like to be kissed. He smells wonderful! He continues to kiss you and you both lie down on the soft cushions on the floor. He kisses you all over your body if that is what you like, or just the parts where you like to be kissed and caressed. Imagine him being so into you that no one else matters. You are so beautiful to him. He tells you how gorgeous you are to him and how much he loves you and desires you.

6. He touches your body the way that you want to be touched. He caresses you in areas where you want to be caressed. …He is

everything you want in a man and you respect him and admire him because he is worthy of it. You sense his respect and admiration toward you. He thinks that you are perfect in every area...you are the only person for him.

7. At this point, continue fantasizing about exactly what you like and what you might have been embarrassed to ask for. The more you see it in your mind, the easier it will be to tell him in reality the areas of your body that bring you the most pleasure.

If you have never practiced visualization, this exercise might seem silly to you, but I want to assure you that it works! It is good to engage in fantasy if it helps to improve your relationship with your significant other...Give it a chance!

Our Powerful Words

> "This is what the Lord asks of you: only this, to act justly, to love tenderly, and to walk humbly with your God."
>
> -Micah 6:8

> "Pain is inevitable. Suffering is optional."
>
> -M. Kathleen Casey

Chapter 12

Betrayal

Abraham Lincoln said that if we want to know a man's character, we should give him power. The way in which we behave when no one is looking defines character. Power is the authority or the ability to control others. When God blesses us with a good husband or wife and we use our power against them to satisfy our sick desires, then God will see our true character and we will at some point have to answer to Him.

Power is what my client, Jeff, used with his young wife Isabel. Jeff was a man who apparently loved God, but his relationship with Him was based on his needs. To everyone around, he seemed like the perfect husband, the perfect father, the perfect son, and the perfect friend. But no one knew Jeff the way that his wife, Isabel, knew him.

Isabel married Jeff at a young age, and he was several years her senior. After their wedding, she noticed that he was what she called "very religious." Anytime things were not going well in his life or he felt out of control, he would turn to God and preach to everyone. At these times, he would not listen to secular music or watch television shows that he considered non-Christian, because he noticed that crises would occur several days after he had engaged in activities that were not consistent with his "Christian beliefs." Isabel had difficulty with his constant changing, because the minute things began working on his life, he would go back to his old ways. Secular music would be slowly introduced, and he would begin to act in a way that she considered "normal."

For years, Isabel had let her husband do whatever he wanted to do. The problems in their marriage did not begin until she decided that she no longer could perform or behave the way that he wanted her to behave. He had a subtle control over her, but she did not realize it at first. He was manipulative, but no one could see it. With friends and extended family, Isabel was assertive and strong, but not with Jeff; he always had a way of making her do whatever he wanted her to do. Isabel became resentful of Jeff's expectations and his insatiable sexual appetite.

They had been married for several years and had two beautiful children when Isabel discovered that he was addicted to pornography. From the beginning of their marriage, he had had an incredible sexual appetite, but she did not know that sex was his addiction. Isabel found pornographic tapes and magazines that Jeff would hide in his truck to keep away from her. He would ask her to perform sexual acts that she was not comfortable with and as much as she hated to participate in the acts, he would expect more and more from her. Fantasies became a big part of his life and he would ask her to fulfill them for him. She would refuse until it became easier to just give in so that she and the children would not receive his silent treatment. Daddy would be in a bad mood and the children would ask what was wrong with him. Isabel participated in his sick acts but made him promise that he would stop asking her to do things that she did not want to do. Jeff would promise to stop, but after a couple of months, his fantasies would become more elaborate and he would again ask her to satisfy him over and over. When she said no, the cycle would begin again. He would be offended and give her the silent treatment and then ask for his fantasies to be fulfilled. He promised her considerable amounts of money if she obeyed him. Isabel asked herself why he treated her as if she were a cheap whore.

During counseling, I have heard the pain in many women's voices when they talk about sexual favors that their husbands expect of them. How can a man be so selfish and expect his wife to engage in activities that are repulsive to her? Apparently some men don't think about their spouse's feelings and what their actions are doing to them psychologically. If you have to watch pornography to make marital sex enjoyable, then there is something seriously wrong with your relationship. Making love should be something beautiful because God made it that way. If your spouse has ceased to excite you and you must watch other couples having sex on television in order to get aroused, it is a sign that you have lost the connection with your significant other and have allowed the sin of lust to enter your life. Connection with your spouse can only be found by spending time and having mutual respect and love for each other. Anytime you introduce pornography into your relationship, you are allowing Satan to have a hold in your marriage and you are fulfilling his ultimate goal, which is to destroy your family.

Isabel had begun to feel a tremendous void in her life, when she met someone at work who admired her intellectually and who wanted to communicate with her at any opportunity available. To him, she was not only beautiful, but also intelligent and charismatic. He went out of his way to make her feel special and important. She began to spend time with him and soon they were having an emotional affair. This man was giving her the attention she so desperately needed. It was not about her body with him, it was about her mind.

A year passed and a family vacation turned into a nightmare when Jeff began to feel insecure around Isabel's extended family. He accused her of not giving him proper respect in front of her family and stated that she made him feel unimportant. Isabel was attending graduate school and believed that he was having issues with her education as well as the many other issues that they were facing at the time. When the vacation was over, they came home and Jeff again gave her the silent treatment for over six weeks. During that time, someone from his work was having a get together and Jeff wanted to attend. He asked Isabel if she wanted to go to the party with him and she was glad to hear him speak after weeks of silence. She said "yes," hoping that the cycle of silence would end.

Clelia SantaCruz - LMSW

During the party, they had a good time, visiting with old friends. On the way home, however, Jeff began his old, familiar routine of asking her to perform perverse sexual acts, and made Isabel feel lower than a snake on the ground. Jeff's actions made her feel unwanted, cheap, and dirty. She wondered how a man who supposedly loved her could ask such things of her. She felt betrayed because he used her to satisfy his own desires. Jeff asked, as he did many other times, for her to take her clothes off while he was driving. She always said "no" and would ignore him until she could ignore him no more. His enjoyment was for other people to see her nude as they were passing by them on the freeway. She knew that if she did not do it, he would be mad at her and not speak to her again, for who knows how long. He would begin by saying that she just needed to take her top off, when she did that, he would ask for more, and then more and more. By the time they got home, Isabel felt extremely dirty – dirtier than ever! She was supposed to be his wife; how could he desire other people to see her, to want her...was she just a piece of flesh? She could not do it anymore. She got in the shower and she cried to God to help her end this horrible situation; she could not do it one more time! She kept asking herself how a man who was God-loving, went to church, was an excellent father, and supposedly a good husband and provider could do this to her. Why did he have to behave that way? She washed herself many times wanting to get clean, but the dirty feeling was not on her skin, it was deeper than that. It was in her soul and could not be cleansed with soap and water.

She came out of the shower and he was waiting for her in bed with his bag of what he called "toys," ready to perform his kinky acts. Isabel remembers getting sick to her stomach; she felt as if she could just throw up. She told him, "I am your wife; you are supposed to love me not use me like you do. I can't do this anymore. I am leaving you." Jeff could not believe what she was saying. They argued for a while and he accused her of having an affair with one of her girlfriends. He told her that he thought that she was a lesbian. Isabel had been spending lots of time with her good friend, Laura, who was like a sister to her. Laura was a true friend who had been there for her in times of need. And during the last few years, there were many times of need. She told him "No, I am not a lesbian; you just make me sick." She left Jeff behind and called on that good old friend from work who she thought admired her and loved her. Her friend was more than happy to hear that she finally made the decision to leave Jeff. His door was wide open to receive her.

Isabel now believes that her life with Jeff was completely unbalanced. Instead of allowing him to abuse her sexually and emotionally, she should have set boundaries. When we deal with sexual addicts, change only takes place when they are caught or they are threatened with a big loss. Instead of confronting his behavior and forcing him to make some changes, she decided to obtain validation from another man. She believes that she should have turned to God and allowed Him to give her the wisdom to deal with her situation. Jeff and Isabel's relationship was certainly in trouble, but they both loved God. They had chosen to walk far behind Him, but He was right there in their midst.

Isabel felt during their entire marriage that Jeff's expression of love during intimate moments was non-existent. They had plenty of sex, but did not make love. He wanted her to do things that she did not desire, acts that made her feel used as an object. When we have sex with our husbands without expressing love, it will create resentment instead of a loving response. A woman must trust that her husband loves her and respects her in order to respond sexually to him. If a woman believes that she can trust her husband, she will feel comfortable enough to let him know what pleases her sexually.

Ephesians 5:28-29 states, "In this same way, husbands ought to love their wives as their own bodies. He who loves his wife loves himself." Isabel believes that pornography was to blame for the way in which Jeff used her body during sex. She could not help but feel that he did not love her the way that he loved himself. During sex, he would ask her if she wanted a big black man on top of her. She detested hearing such a thing and to her amazement, the power of his words came to pass when she found herself in the arms of an African American male with whom she worked. She began a relationship with him after her separation from Jeff and the relationship kept her from turning to God and working to heal her marriage. Isabel believes that if she had been walking closely with God, her marriage would not have ended. She could have seen the temptation that Satan was placing in front of her and recognized it for what it was. She knows that God could have healed her marriage if she had turned it over to him. At the time, she thought that God was on her side because she felt peace around her new lover. She was blinded and could not see the errors of her ways. But she soon found out that her whole life was upside down and that the ramifications of her decision would impact many years of her life.

Isabel divorced Jeff and left everything behind. A few years later, she married a man with the opposite personality of her ex-husband. Many years have passed and she has grown tremendously in her spiritual walk. Today she is aware that when we allow others to force us into acts that are contrary to our beliefs, we create an incredible amount of resentment. We must stand for what we believe and set boundaries with others. We must be mature adults and accept responsibility for our actions, because our actions – whether positive or negative – will affect others.

"Anxiety does not empty tomorrow of it sorrows, but only empties today of its strength."

-Charles Spurgeon

"Worrying about something that may never happen is like paying interest on money you may never borrow."

-Unknown

Chapter 13

The Paralyzing Power of Fear

Fear keeps us from moving forward and realizing our potential. Many of us miss great opportunities in our lives because we are fearful of failure or rejection and therefore we block the blessing that God intended us to have. The Bible tells us that "God has not given us the Spirit of fear, but of power, and love, and of sound mind." 2 Timothy 1:7. Paul, in his letter to the Romans, stated that "We have not received the Spirit of bondage or slavery again to fear; but we have received the Spirit of adoption or sonship, whereby we cry Abba, Father." Romans 8:15.

When we experience fear in any area of our lives, we need to remember that it is a weapon used by Satan to keep us from succeeding in certain areas of our lives. Fear is a learned behavior. We might have learned fear by watching our parents react a certain way or speak fear-filled words about their situations or circumstances. Sometimes we become fearful due to a certain experience that we suffered. We must realize that because something negative happened to us before does not mean that it is going to happen again. It will only happen again if we continue thinking about it and attracting it to our lives. We have all experienced negative situations in our lives and will probably experience fearful situations again, but what we do with our experiences will determine the quality of our futures. When we go through a negative situation that brings fear into our lives, we must see what the lesson is in that particular experience. We must then learn from the lesson in order to react a different way the next time.

Many other things can mask fear. Jealousy is a form of fear; worrying, complaining, and even some illnesses are caused by fear. If your place of employment is filled with people who complain, criticize, and speak negatively about everything, then you need to do something about that situation. Living day to day in a negative atmosphere will affect you tremendously, especially if you don't even realize what is happening. Some people live with negative husbands or wives and are surrounded by negative relatives. Begin to look around you; if during the day you hear more negative comments than positives, then you need to do something about your situation. Of course, I am not saying, "get out of your marriage," or "quit your job," or "kill your in-laws," but you do have the power to end negative relationships that interfere with your intimacy with God. If you can't walk out of certain relationships or situations, then you must realize what is happening and begin to put on the whole armor of God. Begin to speak the Word by affirming out loud what it says about you and your circumstances. There are times when we don't realize that the music we listen to or the shows we watch on television affect our subconscious. If we put junk into us, junk will come out!

A few weeks ago I saw a client named Silvia for the first time. Silvia needed help with several issues that were going on in her life. During our first session, we worked towards partializing her issues in order to set goals and make them achievable. She had problems in her marriage, problems with her ex-husband, problems with her sister, and problems with her children. As the session progressed, she revealed that for years, she was fearful that people would not understand her and that they would abandon her.

Her father had abandoned her at an early age and that disappointment made her fearful of being close to others. She feared that if she gave her heart to anyone, then they would hurt her like her father did. Our perceptions are our reality, and when we believe that people in our lives are going to hurt us, they will.

Silvia married a man at an early age because she feared being by herself. Most of her friends were getting married; she decided that she should follow in their footsteps and feared that if she didn't, she might end up alone. That decision proved to be a mistake and the problems in the marriage started right after the honeymoon. The marriage produced three children and when she could no longer stand the verbal and emotional abuse, she divorced her husband and ran into the arms of another man. The new man in her life came to be just as abusive as the one before and she divorced him also. The next year, she married yet again and found herself with yet another abusive man.

Silvia was thirty-four when she came to see me, and she was about to divorce her third husband. When I asked what part she was playing in this puzzle, she responded that it was not her fault and that she preferred to be by herself at this point in her life. She had started attending church and felt that God could be the answer to her problems. I told her that Jesus is always the answer to any problems, but that we must work on changing our thoughts, our attitudes, and our behaviors. We must also apply His principles and have a personal relationship with Him. Just because we start going to church and having a personal relationship with Christ, does not mean that our problems go away.

Christ does not come down from heaven and fix things for us; we must take responsibility for our actions and make the necessary changes. If we have lived with fear our entire lives, the fear is not going to go away unless we take steps to get rid of it – especially by changing the words that come out of our mouths.

When I read the story of Job, it is very clear to me that he allowed fear to enter his life. Job was a blessed man! The Bible tells us that he had great financial success, a great household, and that he was the greatest man of the East. By reading the King James Version of this story, we can see that his son's feasting preoccupied Job. Job would rise early in the morning to offer burnt offerings for his children and say, "It may be that my sons have sinned and cursed God in their hearts." The Bible tells us that he did this continuously. In other words, Job feared that his children were sinning and that something was going to happen to them.

Look at Job 1: 12 when God tells Satan, "Behold, all that he hath is in thy power." All that he hath? What does that mean? Could it be that when we allow fear and worry to enter our hearts, we lose the hedge of protection that God gives us? Let's remember that obedience to God is better than sacrifice and the Bible tells us that we must not fear, for God has not given us the Spirit of fear. Fear allows Satan to come into our lives and destroy the blessings that God has given to us. In Chapter 3: 25 Job says, "What I feared has come upon me; what I dreaded has happened to me." It is very clear that the thoughts we entertain in our minds carry a tremendous amount of power. Our thoughts and our words can also bring life or death into our lives. Proverbs 18:21 says, "The tongue has the power of life and death, and those who love it will eat its fruit."

I related the story of Job to my client, Silvia, and she began to see how the words she had been speaking not only about her life, but her children's lives, had produced fruit that was poisonous to their systems. Chaos had manifested in their lives and she could not see a way out other than closing that chapter of her life, divorcing her third husband, allowing her first husband to raise their kids, and walking away from everything.

We can walk away from the chaos that we have created in our lives, but if we don't make the necessary personal changes, chaos will again appear in our path. Life would be simple if we could just take on another personality, wipe the slate clean, and start again. Unfortunately it is not that simple; we must take responsibility for our mistakes and allow God to change our hearts and see things through His eyes. Many of us become desensitized to the negative words that we speak and we don't realize that we are creating a future full of uncertainty and fear when our words contain negativity and doubt.

Our Powerful Words

To help my client re-construct her thinking pattern and change her negative vocabulary, I assigned her homework that contained fifteen minutes of positive affirmations based on the word of God. She was also given a sheet where she would record her negative thoughts and re-write them with a positive statement. Many times we are not aware of what comes out of our mouths. When we write down our negative statements, we begin to see how often we engage in negative thinking and then are able to make a positive change.

It takes 21 days to form a negative or positive habit. If we want to make positive changes in our lives, we can use a 21-day mental diet! It is really amazing the changes that we can make when we begin to think positive thoughts. It will change our attitude and other people will become aware of our change. Our mental "diet" consists of fasting from any negative comments. Realize that negative thoughts will enter your mind, but you have the power and control to change what you will entertain and what you will dismiss and replace.

When we pray about a situation, we bring our problem to God and ask Him to take it from us. But then we turn around and speak negatively about our circumstance. How do we think that God will answer a prayer when the words that we speak say the contrary of what we just prayed? In Psalm 45:1 David writes, "My tongue is the pen of a skillful writer." The power of our words is incredible and when we realize that we can change our circumstances by the way we speak, we can make positive, lasting changes in our lives. When we pray, we must trust that God is answering our prayer. Proverbs 2: 5 tells us, "Trust in the Lord with all of your heart and lean not to your own understanding; in all of your ways acknowledge him, and he will make your path straight." He can make our crooked path straight because He is able; all we have to do is trust.

Try the mental diet and see the results you get by speaking positive words about your situation, your marriage, your children, your job, and your finances. As you begin to change your vocabulary, you will notice how other people around you are speaking and it will amaze you to hear the negativity in their words. Try to stay away from toxic people, affirm positive statements and spend time visualizing the best for you and your family and you will see how your life can change!

Our Powerful Words

"Finish each day and be done with it. You have done what you could; some blunders and absurdities have crept in; forget them as soon as you can. Tomorrow is a new day; you shall begin it serenely and with too high a spirit to be encumbered with your old nonsense."

-Ralph Waldo Emerson

"Do not be equally yoked together with unbelievers. For what fellowship has righteousness with lawlessness?"

-2 Corinthians 6:14

Chapter 14

The Ramifications of a Bad Decision

There are signs that we must recognize in our mates. If we are single, then it is crucial to see these signs in the person who we are dating. If we are married, then we must pray that God can intervene and make a change in our spouse. Remember that we cannot change anyone, only ourselves. I teach relationship classes and when I speak about the potential dangers to recognize in our mates, people are able to see potential dangers in themselves, as well, not just in their partners.

If you are a Christian and your significant other has no love for God, run! God does not want you yoked together with an unbeliever. You can have a relationship with someone who says he or she is a Christian and be unequally yoked. Or if you are together with someone who has no character, that does not think like you, does not have the same goals and ambitions, does not feel the same about raising children, does not have the same values you have, then you are not equally yoked.

Many people find themselves attracted to or attracting people into their lives who have qualities that are opposite to theirs. Subconsciously, we are always looking for balance, but many of us have no idea what balance is. No one will be able to give us the validation or the completion that we seek in relationships. Completion and validation come from being aware of who we are and having a purpose in life. Having a relationship with the Holy Spirit can enlighten us and give us the wisdom that we need to discern the plans that God has for us.

When we look for a mate, we must work toward finding someone who is compatible with us spiritually, physically, financially, and emotionally. When I say "financially," I am talking about someone who has the same idea about money that we do. If we are responsible with money and marry someone who is a chronic spender, we will have difficulty in our relationship. When I say "physically," I am talking about someone who feels the same way about health and their body that we do. Our bodies are the temples of the Holy Spirit and it is written in the Scripture to take care of our temples. If we live with someone who abuses his or her body, does not like working out, and has a completely different way of looking at life than we do, then we will have difficulties with the relationship.

If we are already married to these kinds of people, then we must pray. If we criticize our mates and force our beliefs on them, then we will push them further away from God. The only option that we have is to pray and allow God to intervene in that situation. Nothing is impossible if we believe; God can make a change in our partner's heart when we pray and trust. We must release our faith in order for the mountains of our lives to move. If we are dating a person who is different than us in any of the above areas, we need to make a serious decision about continuing with that type of relationship, because it would cause misery and unhappiness in our lives.

If your significant other disrespects you, deceives you, or uses unacceptable language when he talks to you, then he is showing you that he has no respect for you or the relationship. When he or she lies and does not take responsibility for his or her actions, you will have a relationship that will bring you more grief than joy. If your significant other has a pessimistic attitude, sees the worse in every situation, can't get motivated, or enjoys attracting attention from other members of the opposite sex, then you must make the decision that this relationship is not for you. If your significant other belittles you, is unwilling to admit wrongdoing, and is not interested in your future or your goals, then you must take action. If you are single, walk the other way and don't look back. If you are married, then you must begin to set boundaries and stand by them. We can practice the love that God commands us to have, but we don't have to stay in a negative relationship that is abusive. Loving someone does not mean accepting his or her cruelty. We can love them and not their behavior, we can lift them up in prayer and still walk away from a situation that is harmful to us.

Remember that we attract what we give out and you must respect yourself so that others can respect you. Healthy boundaries will protect your relationship with others and will allow you to define what you will accept and won't accept from them. When your spouse treats you negatively, what do you do? Do you in turn speak to him with the same kind of language and disrespect? Or are you kind and loving? Jesus' command is for us to love each other and that is a difficult thing to do. But obedience is what God is looking for, and the blessing that we obtain from being obedient to His word can make an incredible impact. The minute that we obey, His blessing will be poured into our lives, but the minute that we doubt, darkness will be at work again in our circumstances.

Proverbs 15:1 says, "A gentle answer turns away wrath, but a harsh word stirs up anger." Being obedient to God's love commandment is one of the most difficult things for us to follow; some of us definitely act like the "fool" that Proverbs talks about. When I pray to God and ask Him to give me wisdom and help me see my husband through His eyes, He is able to make the changes in me that I would not be able to make on my own. Sometimes it takes me awhile to release my problems to God, but that is only because I want my flesh to dictate and my emotions to make the decisions instead of detaching from the situation and allowing God to touch my heart.

We can't change our spouses or anyone else in our lives; we can only change ourselves and the way that we look at situations. By changing our attitudes, our circumstances begin to change. I know it is difficult to be in a relationship where our spouse does not feel the same way that we do, but when we lift up our situation to God, He begins to work in it. Wisdom allows us to see things in a different way. It gives us patience and when we overlook an offense, the Bible tells us that we get the glory. (Proverbs 19:11)

Many of us think that getting married is going to be wonderful, easy, exciting. We will be able to sleep together, we will be with each other at all times, we will do fun things, and we will have wonderful lives. Well, that excitement only lasts a little while until reality hits us and we figure out how difficult it is to share our lives with someone else. Some of us, right after our wedding night, question the decision that we have made. The still voice we hear inside us is the discernment that God has given us to determine right from wrong.

The Holy Spirit tries to communicate with us before we make a wrong decision, but we ignore His prompting and make mistakes. Many marriages begin with disobedience and we then question what happened when we see that things are not working out the way that we planned them. Disobedience creates a gap between God and us, and consequences from our mistakes can last as long as it takes to learn the lesson. If we walk closely with the Holy Spirit, then we can make the right decisions that have positive consequences. Jesus said that His sheep know His voice and if we walk closely with Him, we will know when His still small voice is ringing in our ears and in our heart. When we ignore the voice of the Holy Spirit because we are young and inexperienced or we just plainly want to give into our flesh, then the mistakes that we make can impact our lives for many seasons. The story of Shellee and Mike is a good example of a bad decision that impacted different lives.

Mike was twenty-three years old, charismatic, and fun to be with when he started to give fourteen-year-old Shellee attention. Mike's father was a pastor of a local church and Shellee attended services with her mother on a regular basis. Mike intrigued Shellee and made her feel special. He was much older than she was and having his undivided attention was tempting, exciting, and challenging to her. Shellee was not allowed to date because of her young age, but she would see Mike at youth functions. The couple had a platonic relationship for several years and when Shellee graduated from high school, she saw the opportunity to realize her dream. Mike and Shellee were married right after her high school graduation. Shellee does not remember praying about her marriage to Mike, after all he was the preacher's son, how could anything be wrong with such a decision?

Their wedding night was a disaster because their expectations of each other were very different. Shellee wanted romance, passion, and love, but Mike was not capable of giving what she needed. She remembers the first night when she was awakened by Mike looking at her and saying, "Oh my God, what I am doing with a wife? I can't do this, I can't be responsible!" He then fell asleep while she was still in shock over his comment. She asked him the next morning what he meant and he responded that he did not know what she was talking about. His explanation was that he was a sleep talker and of course, could not remember making such a comment. But Shellee felt unwanted and unappreciated by Mike from that point on.

Throughout their marriage, Mike was extremely critical and mentally abusive. Shellee never felt that she was in her own house. He would yell at her about finding a speck of food on the counter and would verbally abuse her for hours. When she got sick, if she heard the garage door open, she would jump out of bed and begin to act busy because he would not allow her to complain about physical pain or sickness. Shellee felt uneasy in his presence and felt inferior around him. The couple had arguments just about every night. She could not express her opinion; it was Mike's way or no way. "Idiot" was his favorite word to describe her. There were times when Mike could be the knight in shining armor that Shellee had always wanted, he could be romantic and thoughtful, but those positive aspects of his personality were rarely shown.

Mike would disappear for weeks at a time without letting Shellee know where he was going or what he was doing. At the beginning, Shellee would be frantic; she would be worried sick about him, would think that something had happened to him, and would call people asking if they had seen him. Shellee believed that Mike was using drugs because he displayed a radical behavior. At times she would run into him while she was out running errands or working, but Mike would ignore her and not respond to her calling. Shellee suspected that he was having affairs with other women. Mike's father had a history of affairs and a life full of deceit, and Shellee felt that Mike was following in his footsteps.

Mike's parents had divorced when he was nineteen-years-old due to his father's numerous indiscretions with other women. Church members had apparently come forward to tell of the inappropriate behavior that they had experienced with him. Shellee realized that Mike was involved in similar activities that were a violation of the covenant that they had made with God and each other, but she did not know what to do; she was young and inexperienced and afraid to make a decision. Shellee prayed that God would intervene and that her circumstances would change, but the abuse continued for many years. Mike conveyed a message to Shellee that she was not good enough and that he had to look somewhere else to find fulfillment.

During sex, Mike would have Shellee pretend that she was another woman. The woman could have been an adolescent who he had seen in church that past Sunday or an older woman who he found attractive in their congregation. One of the women who he liked for Shellee to pretend to be was her best friend's mother. Shellee was confused; she did not understand why he would ask such things of her! She felt that she should satisfy her husband at any cost because maybe he just wanted to have fun. Shellee was young and inexperienced. Her confusion came not only from the actions of her husband, but the actions of her own father-in-law, as well. He would use his position of authority to seduce Shellee in ways that would leave her wondering what to do next. She did not have direction or support from anyone around. She could not talk to her parents because they would not understand and besides, she did not want them involved. She was a beautiful young girl and it seemed that everyone around her wanted to use her. She had a heart for God and she prayed for wisdom and strength. Looking back, she remembers God being in the midst of her confusion, in the midst of her loneliness.

Some of Mike's behaviors were familiar to Shellee. He was quiet and secretive, and would not allow her to penetrate the bars around his heart. The charismatic personality that she had once known began to diminish when he was around her. He became a rude, controlling individual who would rule as if he made no mistakes. If Shellee violated one of his many rules or boundaries, then she would be punished mentally and emotionally. He gave her the old familiar silent treatment; the one she had received her entire life from her mother.

Many times we meet someone for the first time and we are inexplicably drawn or repelled by them. We feel strong emotions for some people and react to them as if they were familiar to us. We may make assumptions or draw inferences about a particular person based on our experience with a past significant other. Mike reminded Shellee of her mother, he had that familiar feeling. Shellee's mother was a good wife and a good mother. Her children's physical needs were met at all times, but discussion of feelings or communication of emotional needs were non-existent. Shellee's mother did not know how to deal with anger, pain, or rejection in any way besides ignoring her significant others and not speaking to them.

Her mother's passive aggressive attitude was a difficult thing for Shellee because she did not learn to express her feelings and deal with life stressors. Due to the stress in her life, she developed intercellular pneumonia, which triggered the acute asthma that she had while she was a child. The medications that she had to take to alleviate her symptoms would make her tired. Mike complained about her lack of energy and would demand from her what she could not give. He expected her to have high energy at all times and to serve his needs, but she was not able to fulfill his desires, which caused additional problems between them.

The problems with Mike continued and Shellee visited with her father-in-law, the pastor of their church, hoping to receive counseling. He did not help her nor did the elders of the church. They did not see anything wrong with her situation or maybe did not believe what she was saying about her husband. Shellee was sent away without guidance or counsel. She prayed to God to reveal to her the truth about her marriage. She felt as if she were going crazy. She did not believe in divorce and could not communicate her feelings to anyone, not even her parents. Shellee was desperate to find answers; she wanted understanding about Mike's behavior. The answer came to her when she found that he was having an affair with one of his best friends' wife. Shellee began to notice the way that they interacted with one another, the way Mike would look at their friend, Pam. Mike and Pam seemed to have a connection; they silently flirted with each other, hoping that no one would discover the chemistry that they shared. Shellee longed to have that same connection with her husband, but instead she received insults and criticism.

Shellee began to notice Mike's terrible jealousy anytime she looked at someone or talked to anyone. Mike wanted to control every aspect of her life and she began to understand that it was his own guilt that projected that kind of behavior. He would accuse her of things that she was not doing and she wondered why he would do such a thing. When we constantly accuse others of committing wrongs, it could be a reflection of our behavior and not of theirs. Many people don't realize that we mirror each other and project our fears or any other emotions that we experience ourselves. If our mates are constantly accusing us of wrongdoings, then it could be a reflection of their own actions.

After suffering from several years of abuse, Shellee separated from Mike for two years. She was willing to go to counseling outside of the church and forgive his infidelity. She prayed, fasted, and believed that God could heal her marriage. All she ever wanted was to be loved by her husband, have children, and be a great mother and wife. Mike participated in two counseling sessions, but did not show up for the rest, letting her know once more that he was not invested in the relationship. Shellee and Mike were divorced before their ten-year anniversary, but his abuse did not end completely. He continued abusing her mentally by making threats, having people follow her, and harassing her, while at the same time begging her to go back to him. Shellee left the marriage with no possessions. Mike kept their home and everything in it. He even took from her a settlement that she had obtained from an automobile accident where she was injured. She finally moved away to another city in order to end the chaos and abuse that her fist love was making her endure.

Shellee believes that God was right there in the midst of her ordeal, but at the time, she could not feel His presence. Looking back, she knows that she kept her sanity because God was in control of her life. Shellee believes that she did everything that she could to save her marriage, but marriages can only be healed when both partners are willing to seek God at the same pace. Both partners must be open and willing to see each other through The Father's eyes.

Many years have passed since Shellee divorced Mike. This couple did not have the necessary tools to make their marriage work. Shellee prayed daily that God would give her the strength to deal with the problems at home, but Mike continued violating their marriage vows. Mike left the church when they began to have problems; he felt as if people in the congregation were siding with Shellee. She believes that he was a product of his childhood, growing up as a pastor's son and having to meet expectations from others that at times were unreachable. His parents experienced a lot of conflict in their relationship, and witnessing their unhappiness probably impacted his life. Mike was a rebellious young man who found himself unwilling to be responsible in his own marriage. A precious, young girl got hurt in the process and the decisions that were made changed the course of their lives. Shellee is a wonderful, strong, committed woman of God; she has remained single and desires to be what God wants her to be. She would like to one day re-marry and have children. Her relationship with Christ has risen to a new level and she believes that in time God will bring the right person into her life.

Clelia SantaCruz - LMSW

Our Powerful Words

"I have fought the good fight, I have finished the race,
I have kept the faith."

-2 Timothy 4:7

"There came a time when the risk to remain tight in the bud was more painful than the risk it took to blossom."

-Anais Nin

Chapter 15

God Had Other Plans
The story of Dan and Becky Dean

Someone recently sent me an email that talked about the four things that we can't recover: The stone after it is thrown; the word after it is said; the occasion after the loss; and the time after it is gone. Some of us look back at the mistakes and failures of our lives and say, "If I knew then what I know now, then my life would have turned out differently." There is no way out of the pits that we foolishly dig, but God's mercy is sufficient. We can learn from our mistakes and go on with life because God will give us many opportunities to put into practice the lessons that we have learned. Some of us have been foolish and have gotten lost in our journey, others have stayed on the path that God created for them and are able to look back and see His hand during times of trial and tribulation. In the midst of negative circumstances, some of us tend to run away from our problems or ignore them all together. At times we think that the problems will go away by themselves, but unaddressed issues seldom go away on their own. By the time we address them, the small hurdle has turned into a mountain that brings confusion and stress into our lives. Marital problems can affect every area of our lives and if left unresolved, they can impact us not only emotionally, but physically and spiritually, as well.

It is God's will that we love each other like He loves the church, but that is difficult as we must coexist with human beings who are imperfect like we are. He ordained marriage for our blessing and if we follow His principles and obey His commands we can experience the kind of marriage that we were intended to have. A troubled relationship seldom becomes a success on its own; we must follow God's original plan and sometimes we must seek outside help. Marriage counseling can be an extremely helpful investment in our relationship. When we seek help at the beginning of our conflicts, we are able to make positive changes. Many couples wait until their marriage is on the brink of divorce to talk to a professional. When couples come to my office for counseling, one of them is usually ready to move on and begin a new life, separate from their spouse. At times, it might seem that there is no hope left, but I have seen God move in miraculous ways when couples commit their marriage to God.

Psalm 37:5 says, "Commit your way to The Lord, trust also in Him and He should bring it to pass." We have to surrender our marriages and keep our eyes focused in the truth of His word. When our marriages or relationships with our significant others have turned sour and we no longer have the joy that we once had, then we must look up to heaven and ask God to intervene; we must not entertain negative thoughts about ending our relationship. Many of us have been programmed from early on to think that if things are not working out, then we can bail out. Love is a decision, it is not just a feeling, and success requires both partners to become aware of their issues and work toward a resolution.

Resolution is not easy; during our times of trial, the words that we speak and the actions that we take can negatively impact the way that we feel about each other. After years of experiencing marital problems, we find that one partner is willing to work on the issues, but the other one has allowed anger to build up to a dangerous level and has closed his or her spirit toward their significant other. Anger will poison our attitude and interfere with our decisions. Many of us become tired of fighting and believe that there is no love left for another battle, but we cannot allow our flesh to dictate the way that we feel. Marriage is a covenant

Our Powerful Words

that we make with our significant other and with God. Ecclesiastes 4:12 reminds us that, "A cord of three strands is not quickly broken." This gives me a vision of a man and his wife with God in the middle. Nothing can come against us when God is in the center of our lives.

The story of Dan and Becky Dean is a great example of what God can do in a marriage. At one point in their lives, their marriage seemed doomed and destined for destruction, but God's plans prevailed. I met Pastor Dan several years ago at a friend's house. Everyone had great things to say about him. My first impression of him was positive; he seemed down to earth and easy going. Members of Dan's congregation invited my husband and me to his church and we decided to visit. During the service, we felt the presence of the Holy Spirit and decided that Heartland would be our church.

Pastor Dan is a great teacher; he inspires people to make positive changes in their lives. Everyone who attends his church can feel the love that he pours into his congregation. He is genuine, caring, loving, and funny and his non-judgmental attitude makes one feel accepted. His musical talent is extraordinary and hearing him sing is an absolute blessing to his congregation. Dan belongs to the famous musical group, Phillips, Craig and Dean (PCD). Their music is heard all over United States and Canada and they have received numerous Dove Awards. Their success has been incredible and they give praise to their Lord and Savior, Jesus Christ. Talking to Dan Dean and seeing his humble spirit has been an inspiration in my life.

His wife, Becky Dean, can be described as an amazing woman. She is transparent and I admire her ability to say what's on her mind in a clear and loving way. She shows strength, compassion, and love to everyone around her. I have been told that as a mother, she is the best that any child could ever hope to have. She encourages growth, accepts her children unconditionally, and helps them to reach whatever desire or goal they have for themselves.

Dan and Becky Dean make a great couple; they complement and balance each other on every level. They have combined their strengths to help each other grow and make a difference not only in their own lives, but also in the lives of those around them. The first time that I heard Becky speak openly about the problems that they had in their marriage, I admired her ability to be transparent about an issue that most people in leadership positions would go to great lengths to cover up. Dan discusses their issues, as well, and is as transparent as Becky because he desires to help couples who experience conflict in their own marriages. He encourages people to seek professional help at the beginning of their troubles. He gives excellent and godly advice because he has experienced the worst and has seen God do His best.

Dan Dean and Becky DeHart met in college and became good friends. They had similar backgrounds; both were raised by pastors who belonged to the same religious organization. Becky's father continues to be involved in God's work. He travels in the mission field and he is currently the Bishop of Heartland Church where Dan and Becky are senior pastors. Dan's father has retired, but he worked in the field for many years as a pastor. Dan's parents produced five boys and four of them followed in their father's footsteps and are now serving God in the ministry. Dan became a Christian at age ten, but at age sixteen, he had a wonderful experience with God when he accepted the call to ministry.

At age twenty-two, after they had dated for a year, Dan married eighteen-year-old Becky. According to Becky, their marital problems started during their honeymoon. Becky remembers being disappointed on their wedding night because she had desired a wonderful romance. She married with the intention of finding her soul mate and believed in her heart that Dan Dean was the one. Becky's father had been involved in the ministry full time. Therefore, his time with his wife and children was very limited and expressions of feelings were scarce. As a teenager, she chose the same type of husband. Someone who was extremely busy, had difficulty expressing feelings, and had little time for his family. Many of us expect our spouses to be our sources of happiness, but when we realize that they are imperfect like we are, or that they mirror negative traits that we have encountered in the past, we become disappointed and tend to unconsciously blame them for not fulfilling our deepest desires.

Our Powerful Words

Dan also had a picture in his mind of what he thought that matrimony was about. They started their lives together with unrealistic expectations. Dan thought that being married was supposed to be a wonderful experience where he could have a woman satisfy his every need. His idea of marriage was unrealistic and now he can see that they had issues prior to their wedding day. His expectations were not met, Dan wanted a possession and Becky wanted a soul mate. Both had misconceptions about intimacy, which created issues early in their marriage. When we expect our spouses to fulfill our every need, we will be disappointed every time. It is difficult to fulfill others' expectations; mind reading is not a natural thing. We need to realize that God is the only source that provides the validation and the self-confidence that we so desperately need.

Men and women look for different qualities in a mate. Women look for men who can give us emotional and physical security, men who show strength, romance, and excitement, men who are good providers and have caring hearts. Women also have a tremendous need for meaningful communication. Men look for women that can respect and admire them, but at the same time they like sexuality and beauty. Many people marry in expectation of those attributes and when they don't see them in their mate, they become disappointed with the relationship.

After their wedding night, Becky and Dan were a little confused about each other's expectations. They figured that as time went on, things would get better by themselves. However, every intimate encounter was the same as the first one and they became concerned about their situation, though they did not know how to address their issues. Life went on and no positive changes were accomplished because they were not able to communicate their needs to each other.

Days turned into weeks and weeks into months and about eighteen months into the marriage, they knew that something was terribly wrong. Dan made a visit to his pastor and explained to him that he and Becky were experiencing difficulties in their marriage. At that time, Dan was part of the church staff as the music director. When he approached his pastor and told him about the marital problems that he was experiencing, Dan's pastor asked him if he had mentioned this to anyone else. Dan responded that he had not told anyone and that he was there to get help. The pastor responded that he and Becky needed to keep things quiet. He told Dan to go home and try to work things out. No answer was given, no help was available, but Dan needed help releasing the emotional pain that he had been carrying. Instead of receiving godly advice, he was asked to continue suppressing his feelings. Dan went home with the same emptiness and Becky continued to play house and ignore their issues. The problems continued, days passed, and their conversations became more superficial. Communication of feelings and emotions was non-existent; the business of life became an excuse for not dealing with the issues that stared them in the face whenever they were together.

Becky began to feel that Dan did not love her the way that she needed to be loved; she did not feel secure in his love. She knew that he had a deep love for God, but she felt that he did not have her best interests in mind, therefore, trusting him was difficult. Dan loved his wife, but was not able to express his love. They both complained and made demands and temperamental displays, which only hindered their efforts. When Dan didn't get his way, he would react by giving her the silent treatment in hopes that he would get her attention, but his passive aggressive attitude only pushed Becky further away from him.

Every human being seeks meaning. We all desire to have a deep and meaningful relationship with others; we want someone to trust and we need close, personal contact. Women fantasize about romance, not just sex; we must be aroused emotionally as well as physically. We strive for touch in a way that expresses affection. Studies done on couples show that men often misunderstand their own needs for touch and affection and often seek sex when what they actually want is a meaningful relationship.

We all want to be understood and accepted. At times we want our partners to restore our wholeness. Some of us bring a load of unresolved issues from our childhoods into the marriage and expect our mates to meet our every need. We can draw a picture of our partner's unmet childhood needs by listening to their chronic complaints about us, but many times we only seek to find our own needs and not our partner's. When our partners complain or criticize, the last thing on our minds is to be open minded about what they have to say. In order to give them what they need, we must be willing to make some personal changes. When personal changes are made, the benefit is great enough to impact both individuals; when we receive, we have a desire to give.

Expectations and communication problems were not the only issues in Becky and Dan's marriage. They were part of a legalistic organization and their rules and regulations were hard to follow. Dan was employed by the organization and not agreeing with their rules would mean termination of employment. Becky explained that makeup was not allowed and that haircuts and hair color were considered indulgences of the devil. Women in this organization had difficulty feeling sexy and desirable, and Becky recalls feeling unattractive. At that time, she worked for a law firm downtown and desired to fit in and look like the rest of the women at the office. She would use small amounts of makeup when she went to work, and at times she would do the same while attending church services. Associating with people outside of her organization brought revelations about their differences and she questioned many things about their legalistic view.

At that time, Dan was working for a Bible College and one day he was called by the board to answer questions about Becky's "makeup violation." Dan responded that he did not know if she was using makeup or not, but that he liked the way that she looked. When Dan got home and told Becky about his meeting with the board members and his response to their makeup accusation, she was pleased with his comment. But their marital issues were so great at that time that she needed more from him than one positive comment.

When we spend too much time in other activities, our personal relationships will suffer. Dan and Becky spent most of their time working, raising children, and participating in church activities. They put aside their marital problems hoping that they would go away on their own. They were not meeting each other's emotional and physical needs and did not speak the same love language. They did not communicate feelings and ask for specific needs. Becky had no problem saying what came to her mind, she could turn a conversation into a forensic debate, but she was not aware of her real needs, she just knew that she was unhappy. They both knew that something was missing but were unable to identify their true desires and put them into words.

The church encouraged women to support their husbands and not ask questions. Becky felt as if her whole life revolved around Dan's activities and desire; she began to lose her identity and resent him. She questioned the support that women in her organization gave their husbands. The other women did not ask any questions and did as they were told. But what about their feelings? She recalls that men in their organization were self-centered and that they did not even realize it. Everyone acted the same way and women were supposed to accept it. Becky experienced resentment and confusion about her needs not being met and she wanted answers. She began to ask questions and as a result was labeled a rebel by other members of her organization. Her questions were not answered and she was chastised for her comments. Becky's feelings were a mixture of guilt and anger, she felt as if something was wrong with her for feeling that way. According to the teachings of their organization, rebellious people like her did not go to heaven. Becky was angry at the organization, she did not like their rules, and she was angry with her husband because the rules did not apply to him equally. She recalls feeling no love for Dan at that time because her feelings were masked with negative emotions. Neither one of them knew how to build love in their marriage. Anger and resentment became the biggest roadblocks to healing their relationship.

Still, Becky continued to question the legalistic ways of their organization. Those around her did not understand her; to the elders of the church she was considered a rebel for expressing her opinion. Dan on the other hand, was looked at as the "nice guy." Everyone saw Becky's overt negative behavior, but Dan's covert negative behavior was hidden by his nice personality and his ability to say what others wanted to hear. Becky recalls Dan coming home and taking his small television set out of the closet where he hid it in case someone from church dropped by unexpectedly. Members of their organization were not allowed to watch television, but Dan got around that rule by doing it behind closed doors. Becky considered Dan a hypocrite because he broke the rules just as she did, but in the eyes of everyone else, he was good and upright. Her resentment grew deep and the only thing keeping them together was their love for God and the expectations of the congregation. Becky and Dan remember going to church and feeling helpless and hopeless about their situation, but The Holy Spirit would wash away their sadness and give them enough energy for one more day.

Love is an art and it requires discipline to be maintained. It involves giving rather than receiving. Dan thought that the thrilling feelings of marriage should just come as he had envisioned them in his fantasies prior to marrying Becky. When he did not get what he expected from her, he became resentful. Dan did not know how to communicate to her how truly special she was to him. Tension developed in their relationship, especially in their sex life. Intimacy requires spending time with each other and knowing each other's needs. Dan desired spontaneity in the relationship and Becky needed a schedule. The lack of communication and the business of life created an atmosphere where resentment grew quickly.

Love is our greatest need and when we don't feel loved by our spouse, we begin to fear rejection. Dan was afraid to be rejected by Becky, and rejection is what he got from her. Dan needed affirmation from his wife and when that need was not met he would seek it from other women. Dan was a notorious flirt, and he remembers carrying his flirtiness to a dangerous level. He needed to know that women found him attractive, he wanted to feel sexy and desirable which was something that he was not getting at home. Dan remembers questioning his own behavior and wanted to know what caused his insecurity and his need to feel important. He became aware that flirting did not give him answers and did not make him feel better about himself. Later he was able to crucify that need through education and counseling as well as allowing God to take that part of him that no longer served him. Dan realized that not having his needs met by his wife created a void in his life.

As musical artist and a writer, Dan did not have difficulty putting his thoughts down on paper or singing them in a song, but expressing them vocally to his wife was another matter. Becky saw his silence as indifference to her feelings. Indifference is an enemy of love and Dan and Becky managed to draw away from each other by not sharing in each other's worlds.

The thought of divorce began to occupy Becky's mind. She did not know how to deal with her feelings and fantasizing about divorce gave her the vision of ending her problems. By visualizing divorce, Becky opened doors for Satan to tempt her full-time. Once we begin to entertain the thought of divorce, we allow that thought to impregnate our minds and our souls, and soon we become desensitized to its consequences. One of Satan's most powerful weapons is the power of suggestion. When we give in to his suggestions, we begin to think about them everyday until we have a full plan worked out in our mind. Our plan will consist of how we are going to abandon our marriages, how we are going to support ourselves, and how we can divorce our mates without much disruption in our lives. We have no idea of the disruption and destruction that divorce will bring until much later. Satan was working overtime against Becky and Dan's marriage, but God was greater and He had other plans.

Dan Dean's gift from God is music. His talents were appreciated by many people and with that came offers for employment. Becky and Dan moved to several different places. At one point, Dan was working for Becky's father as the music pastor when an opportunity became available to join a wonderful church in Ohio. The pastor of the church had a positive impact in their lives. He began to expose them to God in a different way. He began to introduce them to a love for Christ with no man-made rules, only principles established by God. He explained the importance of having a personal relationship with Jesus Christ. Dan and Becky knew the word of God but did not know how to apply His principles in their lives. Their new pastor was able to expose to them to the dangers of man-made rules that can kill the Spirit with tremendous expectations that have nothing to do with a relationship with Christ.

Our Powerful Words

Dan and Becky began to experience God's love, but still had a void in their lives where marital issues were still present. They swept their problems under the rug and did not have the necessary tools to talk about their issues and work on their relationship. It would take commitment from both of them to make the relationship work. They began to seek God and pray about their situation; they prayed that He would heal their marriage. They would give their problems up to God, but soon take them back by allowing negative thoughts about each other to enter their minds. The resentment that they carried from the pain and misunderstandings of their past created a wall between them and the blessings that God was ready to bestow upon them.

When we give our problems to God and then take them back, He will cross His arms and wait for us until we are truly ready to release and detach from them. God cannot give us the blessings that He has in store for us when we carry anger, resentment, or any other kind of negative feeling. He has given us commandments to follow and tools for success in every area of our lives, but He won't come down from heaven to fix our problems. He will unlock the door, but we still have to open it from the inside. We have to read His word, apply His principles, believe that His laws and commandments are true, and follow them. Dan and Becky did not know how to claim their blessings and rebuke Satan out of their lives. The spirit of conflict hung around them day and night and they were helpless in its presence.

Dan and Becky moved back to Dallas from Ohio and Dan began work at the church where his father-in-law was the senior pastor. Working with the family was easier because Becky and Dan had a tremendous amount of support from them. Their philosophy about spirituality was different than what they had experienced traveling and working at different churches. They were not as rigid as the rest of the organization. Becky and Dan were happier being back home and she continued to work to help with their financial needs. Still, no one knew that they were experiencing marital problems. They continued to keep quiet about their issues, especially around their parents as those types of issues were not discussed in their environment.

Clelia SantaCruz - LMSW

One day Becky took time off from work to attend a woman's luncheon and listen to an inspirational speaker. She remembers being excited and energized as she listened to him talk about issues that she was experiencing. She knew that she was not alone with her feelings and that other people experienced marital issues, as well.

Dan continued to work in his ministry and Becky continued to think about ways that would help her deal with her unhappiness. She began to think that maybe if she went back to school to complete her studies, it would give her a different outlook on life and maybe some kind of validation. It was summer time and she could begin her semester in the fall. She could get her education and after four years, she could leave the marriage and start her new life. However, at this time, she had two children and school plans were apparently not in God's plan for her life.

Becky began to have morning sickness again and feared that she was pregnant. She remembers crying in bed and talking to Dan about her fear of being pregnant again. She told Dan that if she was not pregnant, she was going to leave him. But God had blessed them with another child. Becky saw herself as having no choices in life; having a third child would add additional pressures and expectations. When she had two children, she still saw a way out of the marriage, but a third child would add incredible pressure. She became more depressed and realized that being pregnant had shut the door to freedom; her plans were completely shattered. How could she afford to leave her husband and raise three children by herself? How could she get child support for the children when she knew that Dan would be fired if he divorced? The organization that they belonged to would not allow such thing to happen, men were supposed to keep their marriage intact and women did not leave their husbands over marital issues. Becky fell into a deep depression and remembers telling Dan that she hated his guts and that she did not love him, that she had never loved him! That piece of information pierced Dan's heart deeply. She said that she had married him because her parents had pushed her into it. Dan was shocked; he had no idea at the extent of her unhappiness.

Our Powerful Words

After ten years of ministry, Dan felt as if everything was falling apart and he did not know what to do other than to trust God. He was about to be a father for the third time and no one knew the difficulties that they were experiencing. God was the only one who could change their circumstances, but at the time they needed immediate help with a professional counselor. Dan convinced Becky to obtain help and Becky agreed to go to counseling. Not knowing where to go, Dan went through the yellow pages and found a male counselor who believed that women were supposed to support their husband without questions. Becky felt worse after the first session because she was made to feel selfish for wanting more out of her marriage. After the first session, she decided that she was not going to participate in something that made her feel worse. She was at the end of her rope and needed validation of her feelings.

Becky continued to feel empty! Between being a mother and being Dan's wife, she lost who she really was. She believed that as a pastor's wife, she needed to be flawless and perfect or God would not accept her. She remembers feeling as if God were not there; His presence was difficult to sense, but in her heart she knew that He would never leave her. She states that looking back, she could see His footprints in the sand, but in the midst of her problems she felt lost and lonely.

Dan got busy trying to find another marriage counselor. With God's help, he was able to find a wonderful, Christian woman associated with the professionals whom Becky had heard speak at the luncheon. Their first session with Dr. Cooper was an experience for Dan; the counselor saw the fragile state that Becky was in and gave her undivided attention because she saw that Becky was overwhelmed with painful feelings that needed to come out. When Dan wanted to interject something about what Becky was saying, she would tell Dan to allow Becky to express her feelings, which made him feel that they were ganging up on him.

Dan left the session and sat in his car, crying and thinking that their new counselor hated men in general, but definitely hated him in particular. Becky does not remember the first session but believes that it was a gift from God; if Dr. Cooper had acted like the previous counselor, then it would have been the end of their marriage. She could not have taken any criticism at that time.

Dr. Cooper made Becky feel that her issues were valid based on Dan's treatment and she was able to point out the negative ways that they had been dealing with each other. When they could not find the words to express what they were feeling, she would give them a list of adjectives or words that represented their feelings in order to help them understand and communicate with each other. Homework was usually given during the session and one of the assignments was for Dan to make Becky feel important by spending money on her and taking her out to do fun things. At the time, money was tight, but Becky did not care. She felt so deprived that she could not get enough attention from her husband. She took advantage of every piece of homework prescribed and knew that it would benefit her. Becky's parents helped pay for the counseling and did not ask questions. Her parents were seeking and praying that God would heal her marriage and help Becky and Dan to see things through His eyes.

Becky's assignment from Dr. Cooper was for Becky to allow Dan to express his feelings without her saying a word, which proved to be difficult because by that time, she could not stop talking about her own feelings. During counseling, Becky found that she was angrier than she thought about organized religion and the fact that women in their legalistic organization were not allowed to express their feelings or state their opinions. During counseling, they both learned to identify their feelings and were able to use valuable tools that helped them on the road to recovery.

The Dean's attended counseling for over two years and Dan was working hard at making ends meet. He continued to sing at every place that would allow him to sing. He worked hard to make things happen. The same year that they had started counseling, he had recorded his first solo album. Radio stations began to play his song and as a result he was able to sell many albums, which he kept in the trunk of his car. Joshua's

Christian Book Stores ordered about 600 copies and that was a great accomplishment for Dan. At that same time, someone from Nashville called him and said that they loved his album and he was invited to sing in The New Artist Showcase. The name of his single was, "I Choose to be a Christian."

While in Nashville, Dan met famous singers and people told him that if he were to continue to sing in Nashville, he would be signed because anyone who sang at The New Artist Showcase got a contract. But the problems in their marriage were still a huge mountain for Dan and Becky and looking back, they both can see that God was not about to bless them with the tremendous success, that they now enjoy, until they had worked on their marital issues. They needed to let go of the anger and resentment that they felt toward each other. When we have hatred or resentment in our hearts, God can not pour out His blessings in our lives. That is why it is important to let go of toxic feelings – or we tie God's hands!

If Dan had begun to travel and sing in different parts of the country, his marital problems could not have been worked out. Dan and Becky were working on their issues, but the road to recovery was hard and long. Dan remembers waiting for the phone to ring with offers, but no one would call. One person, from Word Music, expressed interest in his song. He came out to see Dan twice, but nothing manifested at that time. Meanwhile, Dan was invited by Randy Phillips to participate in forming a new group with him and Shawn Craig that would soon change their world. The invitation to form the group, Phillips, Craig and Dean (PCD), came at a perfect time when their financial situation was at a critical state.

During Becky's last pregnancy, they were forced to change insurance carriers, which left them uncovered for the delivery of their third child. Their health insurance had refused to pay for the baby's hospital as well as the doctor's bill. The financial pressure was interfering with their already fragile relationship. Dan was working with his music and entertaining every opportunity that he had, but jobs were not easy to obtain.

Becky remembers telling the Lord how much she needed Him in her life. Her mother told her that she needed to seek and pray in order for her situation to turn around. Becky remembers questioning why she should pray, but she did so as an act of obedience. One day, she remembers going to the back yard to empty a container of water. The children were busy playing and having a good time, and she remembers looking up to heaven and seeing the sun peak through the clouds. She remembers feeling the awesome presence of God and believes that He was giving her a word, a promise that everything was going to be all right. She went inside the house and felt a tremendous peace about her situation. A few days later, the insurance company that had refused to pay for the medical bills, reversed their decision to pay. Her gynecologist also decided to write off the bill. Those two things were the beginning of the turn around in their lives. God had given them a miracle and a fresh vision for their marriage.

Dan began to sing with Phillips, Craig & Dean (PCD) before their third child, Danielle, was born, but it was not until 1991 that they were officially a group. By this time, Dan and Becky had been attending counseling and their marriage was on the road to recovery. They had made positive changes in their lives and their emotional and financial situations were improving at a fast rate. In August of 1991, they sat on a beautiful beach in Cozumel, Mexico and recommitted their love to God and to each other. It was a great moment in their lives where they could look at each other, experience a new love, and establish a new covenant between themselves and Christ. Three months after recommitting their marriage, Star Song Records signed PCD and with that, they were on their way to fame. Dan calls that wonderful opportunity a true miracle from heaven. Their first album had five singles that rated number one on the charts and one song that rated number three. The company sold 200,000 albums and hit a record. God was blessing them abundantly above and beyond what they could ever imagine.

Dan recalls that while they were playing in a concert in Columbus Ohio, someone asked how they came off as "being so sincere." The only answer that they had was that they are sincere because they don't know any other way to be. Their love for God is what keeps them that way. Dan stated that he, Shawn, and Randy live in a real world and that when they get home, no one is interested in what they did during concerts that they performed because they knew them prior to PCD. Dan has been in music ministry all of his life and later became the senior pastor of Heartland Church, previously known as Christ Temple. Randy Phillips has been in the ministry with his father for many years, but has now started his own church in Austin, Texas. Shawn Craig has been a pastor for over twenty-five years. Their love and devotion to God has made the difference. They are aware that their blessings come from heaven and their desire is to be servants of God and promote His Word.

Currently INO records in Nashville represent PCD; after fifteen years of incredible blessings from above, they have recorded ten albums, a DVD project, and seventeen number one songs. His group has enjoyed tremendous success, but that has not interfered with Dan's humble spirit. Speaking to Dan Dean is as easy as speaking to someone who I have known my entire life. He makes one feel completely comfortable in his presence.

Dan and Becky remember the hard work that it took to make their marriage the success that it is today. Their love for God, their commitment for one another, and a good, Christian counselor made it happen. They remember praying that the Holy Spirit would give them the strength to fight for their marriage and stand against the power of the enemy who had been working overtime to destroy their family. Many couples think that it is easier to give up the marriage than to work on recovery. Satan knows our weaknesses and he will tempt us with anger, resentment, unforgiveness, and anything else that can keep us from achieving spiritual and emotional success. We need to remember that God has rescued us from the dominion of darkness and brought us into the kingdom of his son, Jesus. When we spend time praying in the Spirit, God will reveal to us the answer to our problems.

1 Corinthians 14:2 states, "For anyone who speaks in a tongue does not speak to men but to God. Indeed, no one understands him; he

utters mysteries with his spirit." This means that Satan can't hear what we are praying about; no one else knows the mysteries that we pray, only The Father who then reveals it to us. The second chapter of 1 Corinthians speaks about us not receiving the Spirit of this world, but the Spirit from God so that we may understand what God has freely given us. Our heavenly father has given us the principles for a successful marriage. We must learn to apply His principles and put His concepts into practice in order to have success in every area of our lives.

Dan states that today he and Becky love each other more than ever. He remembers a time when he wondered if their marriage was going to make it. Today he believes that their marriage would survive anything. Their personalities are very different; Dan connects at an emotional level and admits that he continues to have some issues with communication. When Becky asks an intimate question, he can become quiet and intimidated. Dan sometimes regresses to his old patterns of behavior where he retreats to his cave and stays there until he feels safe to come out. But now he remembers that he has learned techniques that can help him in times of trouble. As couples we need to create a safe and nurturing atmosphere where we can communicate openly and effectively with our partner with no fear of confrontation and we should feel secure in their love.

Becky can say exactly what's on her mind and she does on a regular basis. Becky is goal driven and others can confuse her strong personality with aggression, but her love for God is real and her desire to do what is right in God's eyes guides her life. God places people together for a reason, and Dan and Becky complement each other in a beautiful way. They have learned to appreciate their differences. They have small conflicts like any other couple, but now they have the tools to work on problems as they come up and allow the grace of God to change their circumstances.

During the early years of marriage, Becky and Dan had forgotten how to have fun together. Today they have fun! Balancing a life with their devotion to God, their three wonderful children, a Spirit-filled church, and an extremely successful music career, they enjoy life to the fullest. Their oldest son, Dusty, is an incredible young man who is following in his father's footsteps. Dusty is pastor of student ministries at his father's church and a natural when it comes to preaching the word of God. Dusty has a true gift from above; his teaching is inspiring, fresh, funny, and full of life. He was recently married to beautiful Kendra Kelly, who is also extremely gifted and works as a singer for Daystar. Dan and Becky's middle child, Devin, is a talented musician. He has a humble spirit and God blessed him with a voice from heaven. Their youngest child, Danielle, is a beautiful girl who has her mother's personality and a gift for writing music as well as singing. The Deans have been blessed with talented children and a wonderful extended family.

When it comes to their differences in personalities, Dan and Becky view their differences not as a source of conflict, but as an opportunity for growth. They are wonderful people who have a true love for God that shows in every aspect of their lives. Becky states that she has learned to give and take in their relationship and realizes that in the past, she magnified Dan's faults. She is aware that she only has the power to change herself, but that God has the power to change anything in their lives if they have faith in His word. Becky has learned that love to her husband means affection and intimacy, but more than physical intimacy, he desires to feel important in her life, not just as an item on her checklist. Becky is a schedule-driven person and her organizational skills are a wonderful asset, but she knows the importance of throwing away the checklist and being spontaneous at times in order to please her husband.

Dan has learned that loving his wife means to have time and meaningful conversations. Dan's busy schedule leaves him depleted of both, but he knows the importance of meeting her needs and does his best to satisfy her. He has learned to appreciate what he calls "her incredible gifts." He seeks her opinion because she is able to see things in a different way and that provides balance in their lives. There is one area where Dan considers them unbalanced and that is about the love for sports. Dan prays that Becky will see the light one day and join him in

"Football Sunday Paradise." I informed him that he might be asking too much of God.

Our Powerful Words

"Each day we make deposits in the memory banks of our children."

-Charles Swindoll

Chapter 16

Putting Our Pasts Behind Us

When I talk to people about meditating and visualizing God's promises in their lives, it is funny when I hear that they don't know how to do such a thing. People don't realize that they are meditating daily when they entertain negative thoughts in their minds. Worry is a form of meditation, and many people worry quite well. Instead of focusing on our problems and worrying about things that are out of our control, we must become proactive and make necessary changes within ourselves. When we begin to speak positive statements about our circumstances instead of making negative comments, then the circumstances around us can change. Speaking God's promises about our situation gives us hope and when we have hope our attitude about a specific situation will change.

We must pay attention to what comes out of our mouths; when we guard what we say, we will keep ourselves from calamity. If we believe in the promises of God, then we can live our lives as if we already have the answers to our problems. If your spouse does not know the blessings that God has promised to His children, then you need to claim them for him or her. If your spouse continues behaving as if he or she does not want to be married, then remember that our enemy, Satan, has a plan for the destruction of our families. Don't allow him to take your family from you. He is here to kill, deceive, and destroy and it is up to you to stop him from achieving his ultimate goal. I fell under Satan's temptations and, through a series of bad decisions, lost my family. I became confused about what was important and became self-absorbed. The same demon that was operating in my life at the time was operating in my husband, Alex's, life as well. He had a great family, but he became confused and prioritized the wrong things in his life. Just like me, through a series of bad decisions, he gave in to the temptations placed before him.

Alex married a woman named Robin who loved the Lord and knew the importance of having a personal relationship with Christ. He was twenty-four years old when he met Robin; they dated for about one year and decided to get married. Alex and Robin were married for fourteen years and produced a beautiful child who they named Gabriel. Today that beautiful child is following in his father's footsteps and serving our country as a United States Marine. His parents are extremely proud of his decision. We know that his parent's divorce caused him great pain, but he allowed God to rule his life and use him to impact others. Gabriel is a great person with a heart of gold.

Alex and Robin attended church sporadically in the early years of their marriage. As time passed, they began to experience problems in their relationship. Robin suggested that they should become more involved in church in order to fight against the Spirit of conflict that seemed to have entered their marriage. They joined a local church and Alex told her that he would attend, but he was not about to become a "Bible thumping, religious fanatic." He states that he had a preconceived idea that Christians were nerds and boring. Soon after joining the church, Alex was surprised to see that not all Christians were boring, but some were actually "pretty cool."

Alex states that attending church saved their marriage temporarily, but when they got comfortable, he quit seeking the Lord daily. Eventually they allowed Satan to bring strife back into their marriage. Alex began to look outside of his home for what he thought was missing and for the excitement that could make him happy. Alex is a fireman and the job keeps him away from home several times per week. At that time, he also traveled often with a part time job that he had in the trade show industry. Robin was left behind to take care of Gabriel. Being away from home and being tempted with different things, Satan used lust and pornography to destroy what was left of their marriage. Alex made several wrong decisions that impacted his life and the lives of those he loved. He became self-centered and ignored the covenant that he had made with Robin and God. Satan knew to tempt him with things that were his weaknesses; he placed in Alex's path whatever he was looking for at that particular time. After fourteen years of marriage, Robin and Alex dissolved their union when she decided that she could no longer stay in a marriage full of conflict, unhappiness, and sexual dishonor.

Alex wonders why it took a broken marriage, lust, pornography, and what he thought was "harmless fun" to finally realize that sin did not bring him happiness. He played with fire and it created a stronghold for Satan to operate in his life. The harmless fun included infidelity and a rationalization that his marriage was already in trouble. He believed that the issues that they were experiencing could not be fixed. It was easier to walk out of the marriage and start all over again with someone else than to work on the issues that were destroying their union. When we think that it is easier to walk out because our problems seem too big to deal with, we are making a terrible mistake. If we are part of the problem, then we will bring the problem with us and impact our future relationships. It is always easy to blame our partners for the misery that we are experiencing in our marriages, but many times we need to look at ourselves and work on our own weaknesses.

Alex was single for several years. He knew in his heart that he was going to marry again because he enjoyed the security of marriage. When he came into my life, however, marriage was the last thing on his mind. We met by pure coincidence; a friend introduced him to me. After talking for a few minutes, we realized that we knew each other from church. We had attended the same church years earlier while married to our ex-spouses. After dating for over one year, we decided to get married.

Alex states that the negative decisions that he made while married to Robin caused a tremendous pain to his son and to those who loved him. He blames his failure to seek God's truth daily for the destruction of his marriage. Love is a choice and it requires work. Many times we believe that we are not being stimulated in some aspect of our relationship and we fail to see that our enemy is deceiving us and that his main mission is to destroy our family. Many times during this confusion, we have our eyes fixed on someone else. The enemy fools us into believing that the person who we are with is not good enough anymore or is lacking in a certain area, but when we look back we can see how wrong we were to believe such lies. We allow the little things to be blown out of proportion, and we concentrate on the negative aspects of our relationship when the real truth is that we are being tempted and have taken the bait. During those times of conflict, the choices we make will have consequences that can last a lifetime. If we had kept our eyes on our Heavenly Father and allowed the Holy Spirit to convict us and guide us through our times of trial, then we would have made a completely different decision. Through God, we can re-capture parts of our lives that have become monotonous or unfulfilled. When we walk in His light, the voids of life are filled with His presence and His love.

Alex states that as he spends more and more time in the presence of God, and he understands the importance of daily devotions, accountability, and fellowship with people of the same mind and belief, he grows in his spiritual walk. Husbands and wives must be willing to seek God at the same pace. When we begin to pray together about our marriages, our families and our personal issues and we know our rights as children of God, then a beautiful transformation can occur.

When we pray together as husband and wife, we release a powerful force and Satan has to flee from us because we are placing God first. We must remind Satan that we know our rights and that no weapon formed against us will prosper. Prayer is only powerful when we pair it with faith. When we look at our marriage and it seems as if there is no way out of the problems we are facing, then we must pray about our situation and turn it over to God. The more that we concentrate on leaving the relationship, the more miserable we will become until we reach a point where nothing matters but our own sanity. We fail to see that it was our own thoughts that created the insanity that we experienced in our lives.

Our Powerful Words

We can't change our spouses, believe me I have tried! But God can and will when we completely surrender to Him. Instead of looking at our spouse's negative traits, we must look inside ourselves and change our attitudes because that will impact our relationships more than anything else. With the word of God, we have the power to replace negative thoughts and to fight temptations to destroy our marriages. We have to trust God with our whole hearts and lean not to our own understanding. People are going to fail us, but God will never fail us. Anything is possible when we believe!

One of the regrets that people often express in our counseling sessions is that they allowed negative emotions to rule their behavior and impact important decisions and relationships in their lives. Negative emotions come from our inability to see change in others. We feel powerless and hopeless about certain situations, we begin to experience negative feelings, and we allow our flesh to dictate our decisions. Making decisions based on our emotions will cause us to make wrong choices.

Robin has gone on with her life and she is now remarried to a good and godly man who loves her and gives her first place in his life. Robin and Alex eventually put their differences aside. They concentrated on working together to give their son Gabriel the security and the love that he needed after going through the painful experience of his parents' divorce. It is sad to see how some parents use their children to punish each other, or to obtain revenge over perceived injustices. Children should not have to go through the pain of hearing their parents talk about each other in a hateful way. Robin and Alex, as well as my ex-husband, Eddie, and I, have realized that the differences between us had nothing to do with our love for our children. We have all made a point to be friends and put our pasts behind us.

Clelia SantaCruz - LMSW

Our Powerful Words

"As water reflects a face, so a man's heart reflects the man."

-Proverbs 27:19

"You have two hands. One to help yourself, the second to help others."

-Unknown

Chapter 17

We are Special in His Eyes

We are special in the eyes of God. When we go through tests and trials, we can feel supernatural relief in the presence of God if we surrender our pain and our fears. If we are experiencing problems in our marriages, then we must believe that God is big enough to heal them. We must visualize our marriages as being successful in every area – emotionally, physically, financially, and spiritually. We spend plenty of time thinking of the negative circumstances in our lives, but have difficulty spending the same amount of time thinking or visualizing the favor of God in our lives, and pleading the blood of Jesus over ourselves.

When we experience trials and tribulations, the Bible tells us that God is right there with us. Many times God puts us through a trial in order to prepare us for something else, or sometimes our troubles are a consequence of our past negative actions. God might not deliver us from our negative circumstances, but He will be right there with us. Remember Shadrach, Meshach, and Abednego in the fiery furnace? God did not deliver them out of the fire, but He was right there in their midst. The king's advisers said that they saw four men walking around in the fire, unbound and unharmed! They also said that the fourth man looked like a son of the gods. Daniel 3:25. God did not deliver them because He used that experience for His glory! This time it wasn't because they had to pay for consequences of a prior behavior. The men in the furnace served God with all of their hearts; they were not going to worship any other god if it cost them their lives.

Mathew 6:24 says, "You cannot serve God and mammon." Mammon is anything else that we serve. It can involve money, lust, addictions, pride, work, or anything else that becomes the most important thing in our lives. For those of us who have trouble understanding why we are not receiving what God has promised us, we need to start looking in our hearts. Where are we spending most of our time and energy? Are we serving money? Is our work the most important thing in our lives? What are we attached to? Do we give so that we can receive or do we give out of the goodness of our hearts? Unless our motive is pure, we cannot experience the full blessing that He intended us to have. "All a man's ways seem right to him, but the Lord weighs the heart." Proverbs 21:2.

If our motives are impure, then prayer is the key that can change our hearts. Our ability to give can be transformed by giving to Him because we want to be obedient. We want to please Him, and not expect anything in return. We must please Him because we love Him with all of our heart, all of our soul. We must ask the Holy Spirit to change us, to mold our hearts. When we pray that prayer and He knows that it is truly our desire to change, He begins to work in us and little by little our desires are transformed. The things that brought us pleasure no longer do so, and we begin to thirst for His presence.

Our purpose on this earth is to have an intimate relationship with God. But not everyone can serve in the same capacity. Some people will go on to do great things for the kingdom of God, while others may not have the opportunity to bring multitudes to accept Christ. God gave each of us different gifts and we must be able to use the gifts for His glory at the level upon which we operate. When we desire to do God's will, we will find ourselves naturally gravitating toward the things that we can do to help others. We will naturally express or develop certain talents and abilities. When we are not aware of our purposes, however, we become confused and will go in directions that might not be right for us. When we ask God about our purposes in life, He gives us wisdom and we begin to discover what brings life to us or what gives us passion. Little things will be placed in our path, and if we pay attention we can see what God is trying to communicate to us. We need to find out what makes us happy, because when we truly enjoy what we do, God is in the midst of it. Do you feel at peace with the work that you do? Sometimes it helps to ask other people what they think of us and what they think our strengths are. The answer we receive from them could give a clue about our true callings. I see qualities in my husband and children that they don't see in themselves. Sharing that information with them could help them begin to search deeper and find their true paths.

We don't have to preach at a church or be a missionary to serve God. We can serve God where we are. I meet clients who have spent a lifetime working at a job that makes them miserable. They never found their passion, but instead settled for a job that would make them money and make ends meet. If we are miserable at work, it is difficult for us to be a light to others. How can we give to others when we are holding on by a thread ourselves? When we do what we love to do, we live our lives with integrity and passion and we desire for other people to experience what we have. When we dislike what we do, we can be miserable and make those around us just as miserable as we are. We can make good money and not have success; if our jobs are just our occupations and not our passions, then we are not operating in the capacity in which God created us to operate. Prosperity is having success in every area of our lives.

If we look around, we find that many people live with fear every day of their lives. It saddens me to know that many of my clients have become used to living in that condition. Some people don't even know that what they experience is fear and confusion. Deuteronomy describes the curses that the disobedient will experience. It explains that the Lord will afflict us with madness, blindness, and confusion of mind; we will be oppressed and robbed with no one to rescue us. Deuteronomy 28:28. Deuteronomy also tells us that we will have an anxious mind, eyes weary with longing, and a despairing heart. We will live in constant suspense, filled with dread both night and day, never sure of our lives. Deuteronomy 28:65. Maybe that is why people experience so much fear in their lives, fear of moving forward, fear of making changes, fear of the unknown. Deuteronomy 28 also tells us the blessings for obedience. If we are obedient to God's commands, God will bless us in every area of our lives. We can choose to live with the blessings or we can choose to live with the curses.

When we read God's word, we begin to learn about Him, His wonderful love, and His healing power. Fear keeps us living like victims – defeated, depressed, angry, and poor. Fear is the opposite of love and as I said before, James calls the law of love the "royal law." If we live with love, then fear has no place in us, for our attitude about life changes completely when we see the world through the eyes of love. We can all make changes in our lives and begin to change our destinies.

I have known for many years that I want to touch people's lives. As I become closer to God, His purpose in my life has become clearer. I don't always do what God has in mind for me. I have spent many years knowing my purpose, but I spend my time doing other things. I have trouble focusing on one task. I like to work on several projects at once and sometimes that's fine, but it can also be a diversion thrown my way by Satan to keep me from my true calling. When we are doing what God has in mind for us, doors will open and we will see the manifestation of our hopes and dreams. God rewards us when we diligently seek Him, and our journeys will be clear when we are in constant communication with Him.

Our attitudes are one of the most important things that we can fix in order to make positive changes in our lives. We must develop attitudes of gratitude for the things that God has done for us. We should not spend our time thinking that we don't have it as good as our neighbor. We must look at the gifts that God has given us instead of looking at the gifts that others have. When we are grateful for what we have, we have no reason to be jealous toward anyone or feel sorry for ourselves.

God gave each one of us a different gift and together we can work towards accomplishing what He placed us on this earth to do. 1 Corinthians 12:4 talks about the different kinds of gifts. I would love to have the gift of miraculous powers, but that is not what He gave me. I need to quit wasting time and wanting the gift that someone else has and start working on developing the gift that He gave me. When we begin to use our gifts, we begin to fulfill our purposes and do what God has empowered us to do. A grateful attitude will bring to us more of the blessings that God has in store because He knows that they will be well received and in turn we will bless others.

As children of God we were made to succeed, to triumph, but many times we can be our worst enemies. Too often we allow our past failures to interfere with a wonderful and prosperous future. As we spend time in God's word, applying His principles and believing His promises, we can turn our lives around and make a positive impact on our future. We are to be a light to others and share our successes with those around us.

Solomon says, "Where there is no vision, the people perish." When we set spiritual, personal, and professional goals, we are working toward achieving the success that we want in our lives. Every step we take can bring us closer to what we want to achieve. We must write down our goals and our dreams in every area of our lives because it would give us direction and increase our productivity. The more specific we are in writing down our goals and how we are going to achieve them, the easier it will be to make them real in our lives. Many times the problem with goal setting is that we set unrealistic goals for ourselves and when we fail to reach them, we give up. We give up because we lose motivation or we are not committed enough to overcome obstacles. Life is full of obstacles and therefore it is extremely important to have a clear vision of what we want to accomplish in our lives. When the obstacles appear in our path, we can learn from them and move on to the next level. We never quit learning and we never quit growing!

Clelia SantaCruz - LMSW

Our Powerful Words

"I am always doing things I can't do; that's how I get to do them."

-Pablo Picasso

"My mind is a garden. My thoughts are the seeds. My harvest will be either flower or weeds."

-Mel Weldon

Chapter 18

Making It Work

After interviewing many couples for this book, I came to the conclusion that people in successful relationships have God at the center of their marriages, along with communication skills and a strong commitment to love one another. While interviewing couples and trying to find what makes marriages successful, I was told by Sherry Ferris, something so simple, but yet so difficult in execution. When I asked her if she had anything to tell couples who are facing tough decisions about their marriages, her response was, "Tell them to wait because things get better after a while." Things do get better after a while. It is sad that many of us rush into a decision to end our marriages when we think that the problems that we are experiencing will never go away.

The Bible reveals to us the principles for success in every area of our lives – including marriage. But if we don't use the principles and put them into practice, it's like reading a recipe, not following the instructions, and expecting the food to taste the way that it's supposed to. James 1:22 tells us that when we merely listen to the word of God, we are deceiving ourselves. James encourages us to do what the Bible says; if we listen and don't put into practice what we have just heard, then we are like a man who looks at his face in a mirror and then immediately forgets what he looks like. In other words, we will forget God's instructions for us and we will not recognize His blessings. When we do what the word tells us to do, however, we will be blessed.

Clelia SantaCruz - LMSW

John and Pastor Sherry Ferris are a wonderful couple who have been married for over 40 years. They did not begin their marriage on fire for God, but they were both taught as children to love The Lord, and as adults they continued to worship Him. I am told by those who knew John when he was younger, that he was a "ball of fire." Knowing John today, it is hard to believe that he has changed that much. I would describe John as a loving, patient human being who displays love wherever he goes. The fire that I can see in him is related to his love for Christ who has given him wisdom, peace, and tranquility in his older age. John is kind and soft spoken and talking to him gives you a sense of immediate acceptance.

Pastor Sherry might be the ball of fire today, she radiates wonderful energy; she is honest, loving, and funny and tells you what is on her mind in a strong and loving way. Newcomers to the church feel an instant connection with her because she makes one feel special. Sherry is not only beautiful inside and out, but she has a Miss America smile that can make anyone feel instantly welcome. Her wisdom comes from years of spending time in the word and allowing the Holy Spirit to rule her life. Sherry is currently an associate pastor at The Heartland Church in Irving, Texas under the leadership of Pastor Dan Dean.

When John and Sherry got married, they did not have it as easy as they do today. The skills that they used in response to conflict during the early years of their marriage have determined the satisfaction that they enjoy today. The patience that Sherry showed during those first years of marriage paid off. They passed the test set before them and God blessed them by moving them to new levels. This couple has a wonderful marriage and children who are successful and who are serving God today.

The couple married January 15, 1966. They met in high school and fell in love with each other at an early age. The beginning of their marriage was difficult, as it is for most young couples; not only were they trying to adjust to their new life together, but they also had additional stress in their lives due to John being a marine with duties that would take him away from his family. Sherry became pregnant with their son, Craig, soon after they got married. Four months into the pregnancy, John was deployed to Vietnam to fight for our country. When John left her side, Sherry was left to face her pregnancy alone and she wished that she could still be in her husband's arms. Separating from her husband was one of the most difficult trials in Sherry's life. John was having a difficult time as well – he was away from his pregnant wife and trying to stay alive in Vietnam. Beginning their married life with separation and the stress of war was incredibly difficult for this couple, but God had a hand in their lives from the beginning.

Sherry did not want to live in a military base and they made the decision that she would stay behind and move in with her sister and her two children. John spent thirteen months away from his wife and after completing his time with the Marines, John decided to work as an airline pilot. He had many hours of flying experience but was not able to get the job that he was looking for. Stress began to play a big part in their marriage because finances were scarce. John had previously been a good provider and not being able to make ends meet was frightening, therefore finding a job became his number one priority.

John decided to take whatever became open and a sales position was the only thing available at the time. After working as a salesman for a while, a friend told him that there were opportunities for work in Pennsylvania. John checked it out and was able to find a job as a helicopter pilot. By this time, Sherry was already pregnant with her second child, a daughter who would be named Carrie. John had promised Sherry excitement and adventure; he told her that he was going to show her the world. His desire to provide the best for his family drove him and he worked hard to keep his promises, but the company that he worked for filed bankruptcy and he found himself out of work once more.

John began to look for work again and interviewed with a company in South East Asia for a position as a helicopter pilot. The job was offered to him and he accepted the position, but Sherry was pregnant and about to give birth to her second child. John informed her about his new position and told her that they needed to sell everything and move to Asia. Sherry remembers that John's tendency to live life on the edge was one of the things that initially attracted her to him, but moving to Thailand with a brand new baby did not sound exciting at the time. John moved to Thailand just as Carrie was born. Sherry had to stay behind because Carrie was too young to leave the country.

Sherry waited until Carrie was six months old to join her husband. Her oldest son, Craig, was four and the trip to Thailand was difficult. After nineteen hours of flying, Sherry was completely depleted of energy and wondered if she had made the right decision to move there. The entire trip was a nightmare, especially going through customs. There she was with two small children, facing a culture that she knew nothing about. After the negative experience at the airport, things turned around and their stay in Thailand became a positive experience. John worked for the company for about two years and during that time, the couple experienced positive outcomes – learning new things, finding out more about the culture, and traveling.

John worked and Sherry stayed home to care for her children until one day all of their plans changed. John's airplane was shot down while doing a job in Vietnam. His plane's engines failed and he was in incredible danger. John survived, but they decided that the money that John was making was not worth the danger that he was enduring. They left that life behind and moved to Irving, Texas where they bought a quadriplex and made plans to make it in the real estate business. The year was 1973 and real estate was not moving due to the depression.

Sherry remembers that they were not living a life for Christ like they had been raised to do in the Episcopalian church. They began to seek God again and decided to join a Baptist church. John had a brother, Robert, who was fifteen years younger than him. Robert had been a hippie and had joined organizations that spoke against the Vietnam War, but by the time that John and Sherry came back from Thailand, he had turned his life around and was filled with the Holy Spirit. Sherry had come from a legalistic background and she was not about to let an ex-hippie tell her what to do with her spiritual life. But Robert was praying for their family and he wanted to convert his brother and sister-in-law to Christ. At first, they did not want to hear about it. But he did not give up and continued to talk about the Lord and what He had done for him. After six months of witnessing to them, the Holy Spirit touched Sherry's heart and she became filled with His love. John was not quite ready for such a change, but God was using their financial problems to reach him.

Robert had a deep desire to preach in Africa, but prior to reaching his sister-in-law, he had questioned his ability to preach. He felt that if he could not reach his own brother and sister-in-law, there was no way that he could reach other people. He forgot the words of our Lord in Mark 6:4, "Only in his hometown, among his relatives and in his own house is a prophet without honor." God had touched Sherry's heart and had begun to talk to her. He spoke into her heart and told her that she needed to put Him first, not her husband. She remembers being in her room and feeling the presence of God. Robert and his wife were in the next room and she got them up to tell them what she was experiencing, but was careful enough not to wake John up. Sherry remembers being filled with the Holy Spirit two minutes after they began to pray. His presence was incredible and she knew that her life was not going to be the same.

John eventually began to pray, as well and God was ready to change his heart. John states that he felt an awesome presence and heard the wind of the Holy Spirit through out the house. Sherry did not share her experience with John, thinking that he would be angry, but she did not know that he had had his own experience with God.

They next day they were baptized and their life together, as they knew it, began to change. Sherry was knowledgeable about the Bible and when she received the gift of the Holy Spirit, she went radical for God. She began to spend all the time that she could with the Lord and completely changed many aspects of her life. John was not quite sure if he liked all of the changes that he was seeing in his wife. He considered himself more balanced in his decision to follow Christ; he loved God, but was not being what he considered "radical" about his beliefs as was his wife Sherry. Sherry got a job at a church named Christ Temple where bishop Dehart was the senior pastor. The church was small; it had twenty-five members and Sherry served in the capacity of a secretary. John did not like his wife spending all that time away from home and in church, and the changes that he saw in her threatened him.

One day, without telling Sherry, he put the house on the market and made a decision to move far away from the church in order to keep her from attending. Sherry conferred with bishop Dehart about what her husband had done and the bishop gave her godly advice. He told her that she needed to follow her husband and allow God to work on their situation. Bishop not only gave good advice to Sherry, but also helped them with the move. John could see the goodness in bishop Dehart's heart and he knew that he had given his wife godly advice. He began to respect bishop Dehart and have a different opinion about the church. But this new respect for Bishop did not keep John from moving Sherry to Midlothian, where she would have to drive over one hour to get to her church in Irving, Texas. Sherry was not about to let time and space keep her from attending the church that she loved, the church where she had found the spiritual connection that she was looking for. She continued attending and traveling over one hour to worship and could not allow John to keep her from serving God the way that she wanted to.

Sherry's determination created conflicts in their marriage and it got so bad that people around them thought that they were not going to make it. Sherry states that they never allowed the word "divorce" to enter their minds or come out of their mouths. That decision proved to be the best one that they could make at that time. We can't divorce our husbands or wives without first thinking about it. Once we allow thoughts of divorce to enter our minds, they will go into our hearts. There is a process before our flesh acts out what we have been entertaining in our minds. Romans 8:5 tells us that they who are after the flesh will mind the things of the flesh, but they who are after the Spirit will mind the things of the Spirit. When we establish a covenant, we must take the decision that we made seriously and not allow circumstances to keep us from the will of God. Being obedient connects us to the blessings that God has in store for us.

Our Powerful Words

As I express throughout this book, the words we speak about our circumstances carry incredible power, they are like seeds planted in the ground. John and Sherry did not allow divorce to be an option; even during the worse times of conflict they continued to communicate and, like many of us, they at times allowed their enemy to steal their joy. We know that Satan's assignment is to destroy our marriages, especially when he knows that God is using us to reach others. We become dangerous to him and he will send his demons to attack us in our weakness. He knows the areas of our lives where we can be tempted. John and Sherry had a covenant established with each other and with God, and that covenant was strong enough to keep them from making decisions that would have been regretful later on.

John began to realize that they both needed to be involved in church in order to be obedient to what God was instructing them to do. He began to attend church with his wife, but the conflicts in their marriage did not end there. God was working in their marriage and their personalities to make them who they are today. John had issues with anger; Sherry remembers him being like "a bomb waiting to explode." It was difficult at times because she did not understand his mood changes. God had given her tremendous favor with John who loved her very much, and even through his negative moods she knew how to reach him. At times she would use manipulation skills along with her God-given beauty to get what she wanted from him. Sherry also spent lots of time praying about her situation and God revealed to her that He was putting her through an experience that would help her and John to grow strong in Christ. There are trials that we must pass in order to get to the level where God can use us to minister to others. Sherry and John passed that test and today they are a tremendous blessing to those around them.

Sherry knew how important the lesson was and also knew that if she failed the test, another opportunity for conflict would come their way until they both realized that God was molding them to be the leaders that He wanted them to be. God was working in John and little by little He began to change his ways. Without telling his wife, he put the Midlothian house on the market in order to move back closer to the church. They sold the house and lost money on it because they had only lived in it for nine months. But God was in charge and He was preparing them for a tremendous blessing.

Today John and Sherry Ferris are incredibly blessed in every area of their lives. They have two children who are successful and are involved in God's work. Craig and Carrie have children of their own who are a blessing to their parents and their grandparents. The entire family continues to attend Christ Temple Church, newly named Heartland Church, under the leadership of Pastor Dan Dean. Bishop Dehart continues to play an important role not only in the church, but also in the Ferris's hearts. He helped John and Sherry tremendously through their trials by being a great friend and a positive influence.

Bishop Dehart and his wonderful wife, Doris, have been in full time ministry for over forty-five years. He was ordained in Memphis in 1956 and has served in churches in LaFeria, Port Arthur, Paris, and Irving, Texas. He is currently involved with Global Ministries where he has an extremely important role and continues to be a leader and an encourager for change. He and Doris have also been a blessing in my life. They believe in my dream to build an orphanage and have encouraged me to follow what God is speaking to me about. I have asked Bishop to adopt me as his daughter (kidding, but seriously) as I can see that he has a tremendous amount of compassion for others and an enormous amount of love to give. My biological father did not have the time to encourage and guide me and I enjoy having the counsel of such a godly couple as Jack and Doris Dehart. (The last chapter of this book is about an orphanage that we will be building in Nicaragua!)

Our Powerful Words

"Only those who dare to fail greatly can achieve greatly."

-Robert F. Kennedy

"Those who believe they can do something are probably right--and so are those who believe they can't."

-Unknown

Chapter 19

Passing the Test

When areas of our lives are out of control, God will place before us opportunities for growth. He desires for us to release situations that are causing us stress, for when we are anxious about things of this world, it keeps from experiencing an intimate relationship with Him. God wants us to grow and we will have numerous opportunities to work on the areas that we need to release. We don't always choose to release our troubles. But situations will come up time and again and we will have the opportunity to either release them or face them and repeat the same techniques and exhibit the same behaviors that took us nowhere in the past.

Einstein's definition of insanity is, "repeating the same behavior and expecting different results." When we choose to repeat the same behavior, we once again fail to see an opportunity for growth, a chance to learn something and make our lives better. We then question God's involvement in our lives and wonder why things don't work out for us. God wants complete control of our lives and the tribulations that we face will reflect that specific area that we need to release to Him.

I have had difficulty allowing anyone to tell me what to do; I believed that I was self-sufficient and my desire was to make it on my own. I have felt that I did not need anyone else in order to survive in this world. I chose a career where I could work by myself and not be supervised or micromanaged by anyone. I have had difficulty with anyone telling me what to do with my money, with my time, or with my life. I have always believed that I could make things happen by myself and have not wanted any influence from anyone else. In the book of Proverbs, Solomon calls a person like me a "fool". But today, I thank God that He has given me the desire to learn His spiritual principles and make some changes in my life. He had other plans for me and He has been teaching me that I cannot enjoy the blessings that He has in store for me unless I surrender all to Him and allow others to influence my life. He has placed trials in my path and I can't graduate to the next level unless I pass the tests that He has set before me. It has been a difficult task and I continually ask Him to show me where I am missing his message. Everyday He shows me where I have failed.

I have had an issue with patience and have had difficulty accepting what I consider negative behavior from others. Of course, my own negative behavior has not bothered me because many of us have difficulty seeing the faults in ourselves but are quick to point them out in someone else. We can see all of the wrongs that our significant others are doing, but fail to see what we are doing wrong. We need to remember that if we see faults in others it is because that is an area of our own personality that we need to work on. The stronger the feeling, the stronger our need is to either accept or acknowledge that part of ourselves. That anger that bothers us in our husbands or wives is the same anger that we haven't resolved within ourselves. I get daily lessons from above and some of them are more difficult than others. Any time that I fail a test, God is faithful and allows me to take the test again.

I wish that He could just pass me based on my recent good behavior, but He won't. I have to actually admit to my mistakes and allow the voice of the Holy Spirit to convict me when I behave in a way that does not align with the word of God. To this day, I continue to make things difficult for myself due to my inability to practice patience with someone else. Some days are better than others, and I am working toward mastery in that area, but boy it is difficult! For example, not long ago, I was attending school to get an additional license and I had to attend three days of training. People tend to sit in the same area everyday and I sat in the same seat for the first two days. On the third day, someone sat in my seat and therefore I moved up one row, knowing that a French gentleman had sat there during the two previous days. I did not mean to insult the man by taking his seat; I just figured that he would find another one. When he arrived that morning, to my surprise he became very upset about the change and began to express his feelings in a way that did not agree with me. He said that he felt that it should have been understood that the particular seat belonged to him and that I had taken it from him. He said a few more things that aggravated me, but what put the icing on the cake was when he accused me of not having ethics. I immediately judged the man; he was misusing the word and therefore I thought he was stupid! I told him that ethics had absolutely nothing to do with seating arrangements. I told him that he was acting as if he were in elementary school and that I had not seen his name on that particular seat, therefore he needed to shut up and find another chair.

At that same moment I felt convicted by the Holy Spirit due to my quick, negative response. I apologized and said, "Never mind, you can sit here." I said twice, "Please, if you want your seat you can have it. I am sorry I took it." I explained to him that the person behind me had sat in my seat, but he was still upset and continued to say negative things. I got angry again when he said "Madam, please don't make me mad." To that I responded that I could care less if he was mad because I was not afraid of him – and believe me I wasn't!

During the break I went for a walk around the school and I prayed that God would forgive me for losing my temper. I felt convicted and wanted to explain to God that I have a problem with people who are ignorant. Well, I don't think that the Lord wanted to hear that because I felt no release, I felt no peace. When I got back, the man apologized to me and since I had received no peace from above, I accepted his apology only out of obedience. My motives were not pure! I just kept thinking, "You are such an idiot."

God can see our hearts; we can't fool Him. But even if our motives are pure, things don't end with the apology. We still have to face the consequences of our actions. I felt that I had let God down. When I got home that evening, I turned the T.V. on to a Christian program and of course the topic of that particular show was what I did not need to hear! I could not believe that they were talking about the power of our tongues and how we as Christians should have enough control over our emotions to be silent. Well, I am very familiar with that topic; I write about it, I teach it to others. I wept, knowing that God was talking to me. I felt as if I had let the Lord down and cried because I realized that I continually do things that show my lack of patience. I asked God, "Why do you give me opportunities to teach about topics that I myself have difficulty with?" I clearly heard him say, "That is exactly why I want you to speak about those topics, because you experience them daily." Believe me, I am working toward change. My desire is to please God and to be a light for others.

God cannot allow me to go to the next level as long as I continue to display the attitude of an unsaved person. I am a Christian and I want to represent God at every opportunity I have. I don't think that people who were around that morning thought, "What a wonderful Christian woman!" or "She is so giving and loving!" Of course not! They probably agreed that the man was wrong in arguing about a seat, but my attitude was the attitude of a child fighting with another over a toy. I missed the opportunity to show love and patience in that particular situation. How can God use me at another level when I can't even represent him at the level that I am at right now? He can't! Our desire should be to change everyday and better ourselves in order to do His will. God has had His hands full with me, trying to teach me that lesson; I say what comes to my mind and sometimes I say too much.

I was working out one day, walking on the treadmill and a man next to me smelled horrible. He had the worse underarm odor that I have ever been exposed to. I was getting sick from it and I told him, "Sir, you smell really bad...I am getting physically sick from your underarm smell." I got off the treadmill and was so aggravated that I had to cut my workout short due to his horrible smell. We were in a hotel gym and it was a small room with limited exercise equipment. I thought to myself, "How can people do that and not care about others?" Well apparently I was not caring about him. I did not feel bad about my comment to him until someone said that they could not believe that I could say something like that.

The trials and tribulations that I have experienced throughout my life, especially the last few years, will mean nothing unless I learn from them. I have to embrace this process in order to make an honest change in my life and reap the benefits that He has in store for me. God is giving me a great opportunity for growth and instead I have complained that I don't have enough or that He is putting me through something that I can't understand. I get up every morning and ask Him to show me His ways and help me see things and people through His eyes. I want to see things in a different way; I want to experience the love that He talks about. I want to be obedient to His first command, which is to love Him and then love others.

The Bible is explicit about the trials and tribulations that we will experience as we grow in Christ. Paul tells us in Romans 5:4 to rejoice in our sufferings because they will produce perseverance, character, and hope. Well, that does not sound like fun. I don't remember ever rejoicing while I was suffering, but Peter tells us that we might have to suffer grief and all kinds of trials. He tells us that these trials will come so that our faith may be proven genuine and may result in praise, glory, and honor when Christ is revealed (1 Peter 1: 6). At times this world does not make sense, but we have to recognize that the trials and tribulations that we face are part of the human condition, they are part of our growth. Many of our trials come from the words that come out of our mouths. Our words carry a tremendous power and will bring to us what we are saying. Sometimes we may say the right things and believe that our prayers will be answered, but the answer does not come. It is in those times that we must remember and accept that God knows best, that His ways are higher than our ways, and that His timing is always perfect. I believe that the answer to happiness is found in what Paul says in Philippians 4:12. He says that he knows the secret of being content in any and every situation, whether well fed or hungry, living in plenty or in want. The secret is to know and to trust that God is in control of our lives. When we allow Him to give us His peace, we can rest assured that the morning will bring new life.

When we desire and commit to let God make a difference in our lives, we must spend time in His word and be sensitive to the Holy Spirit, allowing Him to use us for small things. We can't just wait for a big assignment from God because we might not be ready. I know that in my personal journey, I thought that I was ready once I figured out that He wanted to use me. He had other plans; I had to go through many personal changes in order to be used by God. We all think that we are ready to do the big, important things, but God's ways are higher than our ways and His thoughts higher than our thoughts. He knows what He is doing and we can't do anything unless He has prepared us.

Remember Peter? He thought that he was ready to do anything for Jesus. He was reminded that he would deny Him three times before the rooster crowed. Peter repented immediately when he realized that he had failed Jesus and became one of the church's greatest leaders. We can read in Acts that Peter preached a message that resulted in the salvation of three thousand people. I would say that is excellent for someone who had previously denied knowing Jesus. Peter denied Jesus out of fear of being put in prison. Many of us deny Him by not standing up for what we believe.

There are times in our lives when we could say something to someone, but out of some kind of fear, or maybe embarrassment that someone might considerer us "religious" we miss the opportunity. Maybe we just need to be kind to a co-worker; maybe we need to stand up when someone is using our Lord's name in vain in our presence. Maybe we need to show love to someone who feels rejected by others, or maybe we just need to show love in our own homes. We deny love to our spouses when we think that they have failed us or when they behave in a way that is not acceptable to us, but we expect God to show us mercy when we make mistakes. There are many ways that we can reach people for God, but we miss the opportunities because we don't think that what we say is important enough or we are not bold enough to bring Christ's name out in public.

My husband and I were having dinner with a friend and I was talking about things not moving fast enough for me. I had many projects going on, but nothing was actually moving at the rate that I wanted it to move. I usually want things done yesterday! I said that I knew my mission or what my purpose was in this world, but that things were not moving fast enough and that the next step was not clear. Our friend said, "I know that your goal is much bigger than me, but I want to tell you that you have been a life-line in my life and that I feel connected to you and Alex and to God because of the kindness you have shown me." After hearing his comment, I was touched by it and asked, "When did we do that?" He responded, "Every time we get together."

Apparently, my husband and I had made that man feel special. God can use us in many different ways. We need to learn what God wants us to do and the only way we can do that is by having a personal relationship with Him. What is a personal relationship? Just like a personal relationship with anyone on this earth requires us to spend time with them, Jesus requires everyday time with Him. Prayer is not just something that we do in the morning before going to work or beginning our routine at home, prayer is communication. We can communicate with Him all day. Many people expect to be "fed" on Sundays by their pastor and they think that meal will last through out the week. Our pastor is not supposed to feed us for the entire week, we must do that ourselves.

The Holy Spirit is right there with us, as we go in and as we go out. It is up to us to acknowledge His presence and ask Him to guide our decisions, from a parking place to a big financial investment.

God talked to me about the importance of giving Him a tenth of what is important to me. I am not talking about a tenth of my income, I already do that, He was talking about a tenth of my time. Time is a big thing to me, I don't like going to doctor's offices because I have to wait too long. I usually tell them that I am a counselor and therefore have limited time for waiting. It has worked for me; they get me in and out quickly. Patience is something that I work daily at achieving. But God spoke to me about giving Him a tenth of my time. Just He and I together, where I am listening and He is talking…what a concept because I talk all the time. This assignment was hard for me, but as I began to spend time just listening and waiting for Him, a wonderful peace came over me. I had truly never done that before in my life. I thought that spending time with Him was exactly what I was doing before – reading His word, listening to other people talk about Him, and reading books about Him. True time with God is true time with Him, spending time to visualize being in His presence, worshiping Him, giving our issues, our pain, and our fear, and seeing Him take them from us. When we begin to visualize His presence in our lives, He will begin to communicate with us. I used to get impatient at a red light, now I am glad to have a moment to close my eyes and pray in the Spirit, knowing that He is with me at all times. He has given me answers during hard and difficult times in my life.

The peace of God is so wonderful that I can never get enough of Him. When we experience problems with our significant others, we should spend time with the Holy Spirit, and He will give us new understanding about the situation. It is impossible to spend time with God and not allow His love to change our hearts. If you spend time with Him after an argument with your spouse, it is incredible how quickly you will calm down and see things with different eyes. It is impossible to respond with the flesh when we are walking in the Spirit because they are the opposite of each other. Our flesh will bring unwanted emotions; the Spirit will bring peace and security. The choice is ours!

Our Powerful Words

> "You have heard that it was said, 'Do not commit adultery.' But I tell you that anyone who looks at a woman lustfully has already committed adultery with her in his heart."
>
> -Matthew 5: 27

Chapter 20

Lustful Desires

Growing up in my little town back home, I had no idea about the sin of lust. But many men in my country view women as sexual toys designed for their pleasure. I say many because I know that there are men who are honest, faithful, and loyal to God and to their families. One of my relatives became offended after reading this chapter and stated that I was attacking Hispanic culture and especially our family. My intention was never to insult anyone, but to write my story. To write about an experience that was lived by a child and later seen with a woman's eyes.

My father was insatiable when it came to the opposite sex. I don't know if he was involved in pornography, since I don't recall Playboy magazines being sold in my country or videos being available at that time, but the sin of lust was apparent in his life. I have been told that I have over thirty illegitimate brothers and sisters who I never met. My father had children with women from different parts of the country. I don't know when it began, but family members tell stories about him and I witnessed a few of my own.

When my father married my mother, he was thirty years of age and she was fifteen. He was unfaithful to her from the beginning and created an unhappy marriage from the onset. Being a physician, he had the opportunity to work with nurses, who he usually seduced. He also seduced some of his own patients and sometimes they seduced him since he was a good looking and successful man.

Clelia SantaCruz - LMSW

When my mother became pregnant with my oldest brother, one of her best friends was also pregnant. To my mother's surprise, the baby was my father's child. That action started the beginning of a horrible experience for my mother that would impact us children in a tremendous way. However, that child is my closest half-brother. He and I share such closeness that I can't imagine my life without him. I did not get to know him until I moved to the States; as a child I was not allowed to associate with any of my illegitimate siblings. If I did, my mother would take it as an insult and I would be punished. I missed the blessing of having some of my siblings in my life while I was growing up. Today I am happy that God placed my half-brother in my path and that we have the opportunity to share in each other's lives. After all of these years, I have met several of my half siblings and I can say that meeting them and having a relationship with them has blessed me.

My father had such an addiction to sex, that women who worked as our housekeepers were not safe in his presence. He would persist so much that they would give into his desires. At some point, my mother would figure out what he was up to and would fire the maid immediately. My father would just wait for the next victim. Mom was careful when hiring help and she would become suspicious of any activity – any look or any courtesy shown to my father. When she suspected that a woman was involved with him, she would be hateful toward them, even prior to their involvement with my father.

I remember being fourteen years old and being asked by my mother to keep watch on my father. One day, she pretended that she was going out of town in order to catch him with a particular maid who she suspected was having sexual relations with him. She pretended to leave early that morning and instead hid in a part of the house where he would not suspect her. I took her lunch and dinner to the secret place, and at bedtime, she had me go to my bedroom and pretend to retire early. My brothers were older than me and were out of the house. I was instructed to wait for my father to turn the downstairs light off because that would mean that he was going to bed. As soon as he did, I went back down stairs and hid waiting for him to enter the maid's room.

Our Powerful Words

I knew in my heart that my father was going to do something wrong, but I still hoped that he would change his mind and behave like a good husband was supposed to behave. But he did not behave and I watched him enter the maid's room as expected. My heart was pounding and I was afraid, knowing that chaos was about to take over our home. I was used to chaos, but I always hoped for the best. I did not know the correct way to pray in those days, but I prayed that God would intervene. My job was to let my mother know that my father was in the maid's room. I was to go get mother from her hiding place and we would together go confront my father. I remember crying and not wanting to participate in such a thing, but she needed me to carry out my part.

That night when I went to the back of the house to let her know that Dad had gone into the maid's room, I was not aware that she had a gun. Quietly, we walked around the dark house, being careful not to bump into anything that would alert my father that someone was around. When we finally got to the maid's bedroom, I entered the room behind my mother and there lay my father with the young maid. I can see it today as if it just happened! When the maid saw us coming into the room, she screamed and my father jumped off her with his underwear around his ankles. It was a shock to see my father nude and having sex with another woman.

My mother was screaming and pointing the gun at them, the maid was yelling, my father was shouting, and it was a big mess! Somehow my father threw himself toward my mother and began fighting for control of the gun. My mother kept screaming and telling him that she was going to kill him. My four-year-old sister, Loydette, woke up from the noise. She looked petrified and began to cry. I remember her coming down the stairs, screaming for my mother and a young man who worked as our chauffeur holding her. He kept her from coming downstairs into such madness. The maid left the house and my mother screamed at me to keep her from leaving, but I was unable to stop her.

My father acted as if we had violated his privacy and was very upset. He left our home that night and my mother was left crying and screaming from sadness and anger. He was gone for over one week and no one ever talked about the incident. No one asked my mother how she felt and how she could live with such misery. No one cared about my feelings and the tremendous shock that I had gone through. The scene has stayed fresh in my memory as if it happened yesterday. The years have not been able to erase that horrible night from my mind or my sister's mind. I have asked myself many times, why my mother would put me in that position.

Looking back now, I realize that parents in that era were not aware of the psychological damage that they could cause to a child or maybe they just did not care or think about it. Today I am sure that my mother did not intend to hurt me. She needed help and I was the only one for the job at that particular time. I have no answers for my parents' behavior or the pain and anger that I carried for years over their dysfunctional lives. After many years, I finally let go of all that pain because I did not want to be a prisoner of my emotions. My heavenly Father has filled my heart with compassion and love for both of them. Jesus has healed the pain, but the memories when retrieved, will always be there.

After my father came back home, he acted as if nothing had happened and the whole cycle began again. He continued to do things the same way, and would get involved with one woman or another. I don't know if the curse of infidelity was passed down from his father. His mother died when he was three years old and he was raised by a step-mother who did not give him the love and attention that he needed. He has told me that he would go to bed hungry and could never get enough food in his stomach. No one ever gave him any love and he in turn could never express love other than in a sexual manner. Both of my parents came from incredibly dysfunctional families and I know that growing up without a mother made my father crave women's attention. His behavior toward women caused him to lose incredible opportunities in his line of work and hurt many people along the way.

When my father was a young physician doing his residency, he worked under a gifted ophthalmologist who was teaching him everything that he knew about that field of medicine. My father had passion for ophthalmology and everyone said that he had a great and bright future ahead of him, but he missed out because of his inability to concentrate around women. I heard stories about him from different people, but not long ago he told me his side of the particular story that I am about to tell you.

He stated that after working one semester for the gifted doctor, he fell in "lust" with his assistant. The ophthalmologist admired my father because he was on the path to being a brilliant doctor, but once the doctor began noticing the chemistry between his assistant and his favorite student, he became furious about my father's behavior. This man was apparently romantically involved with his assistant until my dad came into the picture. Indignant about my father's lack of respect for him, the ophthalmologist dismissed my father from his internship and told him that he would never work in the field of medicine.

This particular doctor just happened to be one of my father's teachers at the university and during the final exams, tried to fail him. He told my father that he was not going to graduate. The exams back then were oral, and my father says that he studied more than ever because he was aware that the questions asked were going to be extremely hard. He was right! No one knew the answers to the questions that the doctor asked him. After sweating for several hours, he gave up and failed the exam. Many other doctors and faculty members were aware that he was a brilliant student and some felt that it was unfair to fail him over a misunderstanding caused by a woman. Some faculty members believed that he needed a second chance. My dad was able to fight the ophthalmologist's decision by taking it to the board. After much heartache and stress, the board finally granted him another opportunity to test with a different physician and this time, he passed his exam.

Getting involved with that woman cost my father a lot, but apparently the lesson was not costly enough and he continued to make bad choices. I can tell you many stories about my father's insatiable lust for women, but one that comes to mind is one of his classics. Rooster fights were, and still are, a big sport in Nicaragua. At that time, men from all over the country would gather in different cities to fight their best rooster. Big money was involved and with that came women and alcohol. After a tournament, my father and a couple of his friends stopped at a restaurant a few hours away from our city to have a few drinks. As the evening progressed, father noticed a pretty woman sitting with her friends at a nearby table. He sent them several drinks and after a while, he invited them to sit with him and his friends at his table. The woman who had caught his attention sat next to him and he began to make his usual sexual moves on her. She played his game for a while, laughing and carrying on.

After several drinks, the woman who my father was entertaining decided to tell him a piece of information that shocked him. She told him that she knew who he was and was aware of his reputation. Everywhere he went, people knew him, not only as a great physician, but also a successful cattleman, rooster fighter, and womanizer. The woman asked if he knew her mother. My father was curious to know why she would ask such questions and after a few comments she gave him her mother's name. My father thought about the name and after a little while, he remembered the woman's name from his past. He remembered being sexually involved with her for several months. He looked at his new friend very closely and knew that he was about to hear some unwanted information. The woman proceeded to tell him that she was his daughter! To his amazement, he was sitting with a daughter who he had never known – and he was trying to romance her. When asked if he felt shame, he replied that he did, but apparently it was not enough shame. He made a joke out of the situation and everyone had a laugh about it and applauded him for his behavior. The incident did not change him at all; he continued a life of lust and infidelity. My father's behavior was accepted and imitated by other men. Male family members and friends enjoy his stories and look at him with pride and admiration.

After years of abuse and neglect, my mother finally left him. He never abused her physically, but the scars of his infidelity were too deep and painful. She moved to United States and once he lost her, he finally realized how much he loved her. He was sad and suffered from his loss, but she never went back to him. She detested him; the sight of him made her sick. Many years have passed since she left him and things between them are better, but her bitterness continues to own her and she routinely expresses her anger about his behavior. Today, they live in different parts of the country and they speak and visit each other. My mother says that she has forgiven him, but she remembers every little experience with accuracy.

My father has continued to use women as if they were toys made for his pleasure, but his age is finally catching up to him. My brothers seem to have fallen into the same footsteps and I realized that the demon of lust and infidelity was something that I needed to break in my life in order for my sons and me to be free of such evil. I have broken that curse by standing on the word of God and being aware of my rights as a Christian. My father is eighty-six and lives with a woman who is thirty-one years old.

Recently, I was informed that he had fallen and broken his ankle and I was concerned about such a fall at his age. At eighty-six, my father is full of life and I knew that if he was not able to walk he would soon become ill and possibly die. To my amazement, my brother told me that our father had fallen while dancing and pursuing a twenty-five-year-old woman. Apparently, he continues to display his old behavior and the country's culture continues to applaud him. With that mentality, men will continue to treat women like objects. I believe that God is going to make a difference in his life, and I believe that women, at some point, will cease to accept such behavior. It is difficult to understand how an eighty-six-year-old man can continue to be excited by the presence of youth and beauty when he should be rocking in a rocking chair, enjoying his great-grandchildren. My father apparently is not aware that he has an addiction and therefore does not see it as an issue that he needs to face.

We are exposed to images of beautiful and desirable people everyday of our lives. The Internet has created a vehicle for lust in the privacy of our own homes and now cell phones seem to be the newest way to watch porn while driving our cars, waiting at a red light, sitting in our offices, or any other place that we can think of. No one can see what we are doing, and in our minds we are not doing anything wrong when we spend a few minutes or a couple of hours a day watching or participating in pornographic activity. But that is certainly a lie from hell and it will lead us into spiritual death. We can hardly view a show on television that is not saturated with nudity or sexual images. We are being bombarded at every corner with pictures that stay in our conscious as well as our subconscious minds. Those pictures later manifest as fantasies that will lead us to undesirable behaviors and away from experiencing the intimacy that we so desperately crave in our marriages. Intimacy requires honesty, and when we live in a fantasy world, we are living a lie. Living with lies everyday will keep us from experiencing the love of God in our lives. It will keep us from having a healthy relationship with our significant others.

Pornography kills the spirit and destroys marriages. Addictions corrupt our souls and give us the desire to want more and more, and our souls become a bottomless barrel, wanting to be filled, but insatiable by nature. Satan knows our specific weaknesses and he will tempt us with things that he knows we will have a difficult time turning down. If infidelity is our weakness, then he will certainly bring the opportunity to our door. He knows how we have reacted in the past and will continue to tempt us so we can fall again. The sin of sexual immorality will cause psychological and spiritual damage in our lives.

Some of the leaders of our nation have not been great examples to follow. President Kennedy was notorious for his infidelity and President Clinton was an absolute joke; to Clinton having oral sex was not considered infidelity. These leaders of our nation have had no respect for the sanctity of marriage. We also read about pastors getting involved with women in their congregation. Child pornography is found in Boy Scout leaders' homes and computers. There are sports idols like Colby Bryant with his wife right by his side, holding his hand, while he describes how he seduced the Colorado woman the same evening that he arrived at a particular resort. For goodness sake, he had just left his wife's side a few hours before. What is wrong with our society that women allow themselves to be victims and let men disrespect them that way? Why do husbands sitting next to their wives in a restaurant try to get the attention of other men at the table when some attractive female walks in? Why do we allow our husbands to disrespect us that way? Do we notice and not say anything in order to keep peace? Or do we just not care? We must treat others the way that we want to be treated and I believe that men would feel offended if we women displayed such behavior.

Some of us may play a part in our husbands' desires to seek pleasure outside of our home when we are not interested in satisfying their needs. There needs to be accountability about the part that we play when it comes to our sexual relationships. The Bible is very explicit about sexuality. Sex is a beautiful thing created by God and it should be treated that way. When women withhold sex as punishment for negative behaviors exhibited by their husbands or use sex to manipulate them into doing what they want them to do, they will find that they are playing with fire and at some point, will get burned. Let's face it; men are more visual than women are. They are constantly bombarded with beauty and sex from the media and everywhere else. Everywhere we look, we can see young women walking around half-dressed. Our society believes that having fun should be the number one priority in life, and women come on to men as often as men come on to women. It would be difficult for a man not to be enticed by such things when he is sexually starved at home.

As Christians, we must realize that anything in our lives that is not working the way that it should can be taken to the altar. We need to allow God to heal every part of our marriages – including our sex lives. Satan will attack any unhealthy area of our lives even harder; he knows our weaknesses. All that he has to do is tempt us in that area and if we fall, he has won that battle. We can live what we call a "Christian life" and have the sin of lust in our lives. The affect that this sin has in the church is enormous and alarming. Something must be done to make people understand that sexual immorality can kill the spirit and keep us from having a relationship with God.

As the leaders of the home, husbands must know the importance of spiritual purity and the danger that they are exposing their families to when they allow darkness into their homes. Remember that children pay for the sins of their fathers and curses are passed down from generation to generation. Disobedience saddens God more than anything else. We need to pray daily for the protection of our minds. We need to pray daily for our spouses and our children. We need to pray that God will place in their lives the right people and remove people who can lead them to the wrong path. We must be careful with the things that we allow to enter our homes. Sometimes we close doors, but leave windows right open for the enemy to bring misery into our lives. The price that we pay for succumbing to temptations is incredible. The impact of our decisions will affect not only our lives, but also the lives of our children.

James 5:16 tells us to confess our sins to each other so that we might be healed because the prayer of a righteous man is powerful and effective. Accountability is one of the best things that we have to fight against the temptation of lust. We must make a commitment to make a positive change. Any addiction becomes a journey and changing our pattern of behavior can be difficult, especially without the help of the Holy Spirit. When we shine the light of God into the darkness of our lives, the darkness will lose its power. Satan would like to see us destroy our lives, our marriages, and our relationships with our Heavenly Father, but we can make a different decision and stand against his fiery darts by knowing what God says in His word.

When we have one moment with the Holy Spirit, He can remove anything that is controlling us; the key is releasing it to Him. Detaching from our addictions can give us the freedom that we need in order to get on with life and work on our marriages, our families, or anything else that we have neglected because of our incontrollable thoughts. We can conquer our thoughts when we begin to renew our minds. When we apply God's principles in our lives, we can live victoriously. God tells us to resist the devil and that he will flee from us. Anytime we resist temptation, we are one step closer to our goals. Anytime we exercise control over our thoughts, we get stronger against whatever addiction we are dealing with. When we find God, we can be free.

Our Powerful Words

Some people release their addictions to God, and they pray that their marriage can be put together, but Satan attacks again. When we take the bait, the vicious cycle continues. The weakness of allowing one negative thought can bring the whole nightmare back to life, because the minute we begin to entertain the thoughts again, we have just cancelled out our prayers. I am not saying that controlling our thoughts is easy. What I am saying is that if we practice controlling our thoughts, it becomes easier than the last time that we tried. Just because a thought comes into our mind, does not mean that it has to stay there. Get busy doing something else! Two different thoughts cannot occupy your mind at the same time and you can actually choose what you want to think about.

Some people think that because they are doing what they consider the right things – attending church every Sunday, providing for their families, doing good and charitable deeds – God will not punish them for their sexual sin. God does not punish us! The fact is that He forgives us for any sin as long as we repent, but that does not mean that the consequences of our actions are removed from our lives. Many times we pay dearly for the sins of the past. As stated before, some people don't consider pornography a sin because they believe that it does not take up that much time in their lives and in their minds, they are not hurting anyone.

According to experts, many women have no idea that their husbands are dependent on pornography and are shocked when they find out that the man who they married is looking at or watching such things. When we find out that our spouse is involved in an activity that is unacceptable to us, it can crush us. We can live with a person for many years and have no idea what goes on in their minds and what type of behavior they are engaging in. When we confront them with our findings, they usually deny that they have a problem. Some actually believe that it isn't a problem; they believe that it is under their control. This lie keeps them from seeing pornography for what it is; an addiction that is difficult to break.

It is a lonely struggle for a person who is trying to quit watching pornography; like any other addiction, the desire to engage in this behavior seems stronger than them. How can you deal with sexual temptation? You can turn it over to God and increase your prayer life. The triggers will still to be there, but you can develop strategies to walk away from temptation.

When I facilitated classes for sexual offenders, they first thing that we expected of them was to accept responsibility and the second was to be accountable to a peer. One rule was to walk away from places where temptation could occur and to not place themselves in situations where they would be faced with their weakness. It is the same when you are dealing with pornography. You must be accountable to someone who is spiritually mature, so that if you fall, that person can help you get back up instead of judging you. It is sad when we find that pastors who are the leaders of our churches are dealing with the same issue; Satan will attack a man of God more because Satan's intention is to destroy those who can have an impact on others. If he can attack our leaders, then it will be easier to attack the followers. It is still difficult to understand how a man who is anointed to preach can fall under such temptation, but we all can fall, no one is above temptation.

In order to fight the everyday temptations, we must first pray, and ask God to give us strength and refocus our minds. We do have a choice of the thoughts that we entertain and we have the choice to replace those thoughts with something else. Jesus said that He would give us a way out when we faced temptations. When He was tempted by Satan during his forty days of fasting, He stood against temptation by quoting scripture. The Bible tells us that after tempting Him three times with things that were hard to turn down, Satan left Him. Satan could not tempt Him anymore because he knew that Jesus was not going to fall for his lies.

As we continue to practice dismissing the thoughts and desires that come into our minds, the difficulty of the task diminishes. The more that we practice controlling our thoughts, the easier it becomes and the

Our Powerful Words

more control we can have over our lives. Our flesh is not stronger than our Spirit.

Pornography is not just visual, it can be auditory and written, as well, which is how women participate in it without knowing. Romance novels are a perfect example of how women get tangled up in this sin. They start fantasizing about a world that does not exist and then they expect their significant others to fulfill their desires and needs. Trying to gain fulfillment from someone who does not have the capacity to give us what we so desperately need – which is spiritual connection – leaves us searching for it somewhere else. Communication and honesty are key to intimacy, and many of us live in a world where we don't even know how we feel, much less how to express those feelings to someone else.

The story of Barbara and Kent is an example of a couple who tried to give their problems to God; Kent's flesh was more powerful than the beautiful family that God had blessed him with and in one moment, it was all taken away. Kent and Barbara were married for twenty-six years! They were committed Christians and attended church on a regular basis. Everything about them looked picture perfect to others, but no one knew the problems that they were experiencing in their marriage. Early in the marriage, Barbara realized that something was wrong; she had difficulty communicating with Kent about matters of the heart. She felt as if something were missing, but could not get to the root of the problem. She felt that they were having problems with intimacy because he did not desire her the way that he should desire his wife. When she asked him if there was anything wrong, he would say that it was all in her mind.

The years passed and after giving birth to two children, Barbara insisted that they go to marriage counseling because she could not connect with Kent at any level. He agreed to attend counseling and participated in individual as well as joint sessions. During one of their sessions, the counselor informed Barbara that Kent had something to tell her. Barbara was anxious to find answers that would give her a clue to understanding his behavior. To her surprise, he informed her that he had been involved in pornography since he was a young teen and that he continued to use it on a daily basis.

Barbara was shocked to find that Kent had been involved in pornography, but glad to know that something was actually happening and that it was not all in her head. She felt that with that information, they could begin to work toward fixing their intimacy problem. He repented and she forgave him, trusting that he was going to leave his addiction behind. She had no idea that the pornography demon had claimed ownership of Kent's temple and that the demon was not going anywhere. The counselor assured her that Kent's personality was not the type to have an affair. She also informed her that men who spend time daily involved in pornography, will usually end up having extra-marital affairs, but not in Kent's case. She stated that a man like Kent does not have relationships with real women; he just wants to look at women, but not be intimate with them. Barbara believed her because she was an experienced counselor. However, not only was this counselor wrong about her projections, but she had also failed to explain the cycle of addiction.

Barbara and Kent continued with their everyday lives and things improved for a little while. She tried to concentrate on the positive aspects of the relationship and hoped that at some point, Kent could conquer his addiction. He loved her the best way that he could, but he never got the healing that he needed. Several years passed and they continued with a marriage that had no spiritual or physical connection. Kent avoided being physically or emotionally involved with his wife. On the rare occasions when they were intimate, Kent had difficulty performing sexually. He then would find excuses or blame her for his inability to perform, causing more stress in their marriage.

After fifteen years of experiencing physical and emotional problems in her marriage, Barbara insisted that something was definitely wrong and asked that they go back to counseling. By now, they had four children and working on their marriage was extremely important for their children's sake. Kent went to a counselor again and it was revealed that he had a dysfunctional relationship with his parents. According to the counselor, his unwillingness to be vulnerable came from the childhood issues that he had never dealt with. During counseling, he again confessed that he was spending lots of time involved in pornography. Fifteen years had passed since the first counseling session and by now he was self-employed, and had his personal computer and lots of time he did not have to account for. Barbara states that she never saw or ran across a single thing that would have indicated that he was back into pornography. Kent was charming, educated, well-spoken, and very involved in church activities. At that time, pornography was not talked about and people did not know its cycle of addiction or the danger of such a behavior. To others, the issues in their marriage would look as if they were about her and not him; he was too perfect in everyone's eyes. Kent was attending seminary and working toward his PhD, but according to Barbara, he dropped out of seminary because he didn't want to pursue what God was telling him to do. The sin in his life was keeping him from being obedient to the call that God had placed in his life.

At the counseling session, Kent told Barbara that he was sorry and asked for her forgiveness. Barbara had forgiven him many times and she prayed that God would give her strength to do it once more. After years of experiencing his lack of emotion, she felt angry and could not understand his behavior. She wanted him to love her and appreciate her for who she was. Kent was a good father and a good financial provider, but she needed much more than that. The issues between them were difficult to hide and the children could see that something was wrong with their parents.

Twenty-one years into their marriage, their second daughter left for college. Kent's behavior improved for a while, but the intimacy problem continued. They had grown further apart and their sexual encounters became less frequent than ever. He would stay up late and say that he had work to do. He would go into his office and would stay up for hours to avoid spending intimate time with his wife. Once in a while he would initiate a sexual encounter to keep Barbara off his back, but those times were few and far in between. After all those years, Barbara had had enough and finally told him that she could not play the game anymore and that she was not going to be his "Christian whore."

Barbara asked Kent to move to another bedroom and he did, never saying a word other than that it was her fault because she was not meeting his sexual needs. They lived under the same roof but in different bedrooms for several months. They continued to attend church, showing everyone else that their life was "picture perfect." Barbara believes that the church gives women negative advice, telling women to love and forgive their husbands and not giving women permission to be angry, express their emotions, and demand that changes be made. Submission is sometimes confused with acceptance of negative behavior.

The problems continued and one day Barbara was picking up a prescription at the pharmacy, when to her surprise the attendant asked her if she wanted to pick her husband's Viagra. Barbara had previously found some condoms in one of his pockets and she began to fear what most women fear the most; her husband was having an affair! Their 25th anniversary was approaching, and she confronted him with her information. He denied everything at the beginning, but Barbara insisted that he be honest so that they could work on their marriage. She asked if he would be honest enough to tell her something that he had never expressed to her before. He told her that he wanted to come clean and confessed that he was into sadistic, perverted porn. Barbara was shocked by his revelation and did not know what to do with that information other than pray.

Days passed and one night God woke Barbara up from a dream where she saw Kent having an affair with a young woman. When she asked Kent if he was having an affair, he denied it and said that he was involved with pornography, but not with women. They went back to counseling and after two months of counseling, he confessed to having an affair but promised to end it.

Weeks later, they were sitting at the kitchen table paying bills and a woman called Kent's cell phone. Barbara could see his reaction when a female voice came on the line. They argued about it and Kent tried to manipulate the situation by placing blame back on Barbara, until he finally confessed to having an affair with a prostitute. He had met her at a massage parlor two years prior. She lived near by and told him that she would perform the same kind of service if he came to her house. He had taken her up on her offer and he had been going to her house for sadistic and masochistic sex. The woman was twenty-four years of age – as young as one of his daughters!

Barbara visited her husband's young girlfriend and she was able to find out details about their relationship. Kent had been sexually involved with her three times per week for the last two years. The woman responded to all of her questions and gave her enough information. Barbara decided that she could not continue living a life of deceit with a man who had lied to her for so many years. She could not take the abuse anymore! She filed for divorce after twenty-six years of marriage, leaving her children to carry the pain of a shattered family.

The story of Barbara and Kent is a sad story, but one that happens often in America and all over the world. Sexual immorality destroys marriages and we women feel inadequate when we find that our significant others are having affairs with younger women. It also hurts to know that they are looking at pictures of other women; women who might not look like us. If we are over forty, we already feel as if every part of our bodies that can go south has gone there. We don't look the same or feel the same about ourselves as we did when we were young and considered ourselves attractive. We realize that our husbands are looking for youth and beauty and it causes us terrible pain. It is degrading when such a thing happens in our relationships. During counseling, some of my clients have complained about their husbands being involved sexually with co-workers or younger women. They have found that pornography played a big part in their husband's decision to be unfaithful. One individual admitted to having been involved in pornography since he was eight years old. He used to watch when his father looked at pornography and he learned by observation. It is a shame that fathers can pass this terrible sin to their young children. They don't realize the damage that it causes not only to their marriages, but to their souls, as well.

Research shows that men who feel inadequate about their sexual performance and unconsciously worry about their masculinity, may suffer from acute anxiety that interferes with their capacity to perform sexually. The more a man worries about his performance, the worse his performance actually is until it gets to the point that just by thinking about it; he can begin to experience acute anxiety. Men who suffer from this type of disorder may begin to use pornography to compensate for their inadequacy. While no one is looking, they are able to release their sexual urges without suffering the embarrassment of a poor performance with their significant others.

Women also have many hang-ups about sex, especially when they believe that their bodies are not pretty, or that they are too fat, too thin, too short, or too tall. Studies show that women who suffer from low testosterone levels have a low sex drive. Low testosterone levels can occur not only in menopausal women, but also in young women, or those who exercise excessively, are slim, or have been on birth control for a long period of time.

Fatigue can also play a very important factor in our sex drives. If a woman is raising small kids and working full time, then she is probably exhausted and the last thing on her mind is having to perform at night. Communication plays a big part in this equation because we must communicate what we are feeling and state our needs to one another. We must prioritize in order to have a healthy relationship. But there is a problem when wives prioritize and give their time and love to their husbands and their husbands still spend enormous amounts of time watching pornography and fantasizing about other women. Men forget that they don't have to fight evil alone. They must first pray about their addiction and surrender their desires to God. They must be accountable to someone about their behavior and have someone to talk to when they feel weak. Fighting addictions is not easy, but when we make the decision to crucify the flesh, God will be there to help us and give us the strength to put it all behind. Satan will bring our problems right back to us, but we have the power to turn it over again and not accept his temptations.

Our Powerful Words

"For peace of mind, resign as general manager of the universe."

-Anonymous

"Life is like an ever-shifting kaleidoscope-
A slight change, and all patterns alter."

-Sharon Salzberg

Chapter 21

Divine Intervention

There are times in our lives when we can see that God had angels in charge of our destinies. Times when we don't understand how we got out of a situation that could have been harmful or fatal, but when we look back, we can see that something divine took place. When we have a personal relationship with Christ and spend daily time in His presence, He is able to warn us and keep us from the fiery darts of our enemy. We are able to hear the voice of the Holy Spirit. We don't hear an audible voice, but we can sense Him guiding us and warning us about situations in our lives. In the last couple of years, three times I have felt an uneasy feeling as I leave my house or as I get up in the morning. Nothing extremely revealing, but just a sense of concern. The feeling is difficult to explain, but it's there and it requires prayer and discernment about something unknown.

A couple of years ago, I was conducting a home study for a family that was seeking to adopt a child. I am a provider for Tarrant County family court and I do contract work with families desiring to adopt children. I have to make home visits in order to determine if the family is appropriate for the child. This particular day, I was not familiar with the city or the address where my visit was going to be conducted and I was looking at the directions that I had obtained from Mapquest. I was driving my Porsche, and after trying to read and drive at the same time, I found myself facing an eighteen-wheeler that was coming head on toward me. I had moved into that lane without realizing it, and the driver of the truck was driving too fast to stop and could not switch lanes due to other vehicles in the lane next to him.

I cannot explain how I was able to get out of the truck's path, but I know there were angels watching over me! That morning when I got up, I had had such an uneasy feeling that I began to pray and ask for extra protection. I knew the feeling was related to me and not members of my family. As I got into my car, I felt the premonition that something bad was going to happen. I prayed again and drove off to my destination and continued to thank Jesus for being with me and protecting me. I know today that not a trace of that little car – or me – would have been left if I had not covered myself with the armor of God.

Several months passed and again I felt that same feeling. I prayed again and to my surprise, another eighteen-wheeler moment occurred in my life. This time the truck hit me, but I was able to move with it instead of against it and the damage was minimal. I was again driving the Porsche and it was incredible that I got hit and did not get hurt. I knew that the angels of heaven were again taking care of me. I felt as if Satan wanted me dead, but God had other plans!

The Spirit of discernment is a wonderful gift and I have been privileged to have this gift for many years, even prior to giving my life completely to Christ. Not long ago, the same, familiar feeling came over me and this time I knew that someone else was involved. It was not about me, but I knew it was someone or something close to me. I prayed about the feeling and put it out of my mind. It came again several times and I chose to ignore it because the feeling was a little different than previous times. It was just an uneasy feeling, hard to decipher, and after praying I felt that maybe I was just making it up. Ignoring the word of God can cause tremendous damage. That decision impacted someone who I truly love. The situation could have much worse, but God and His angels showed up again. I will never forget that dreadful night when someone else's life was impacted tremendously. If I had listened to the

Holy Spirit, it could have been avoided; that night, I could have taken control and the situation would have changed completely.

The Holy Spirit resides within us; He is there to help us with anything that goes on in our lives. Nothing is too small or big for Him; He protects us even when we are not walking closely with Him.

Another incident that impacted my life in a great way occurred several years ago. I had abandoned God and was not communicating with Him because I had allowed sin to enter my life. 1999 was a difficult year and I made several mistakes that would impact my life forever. That year, I was involved in an automobile accident, walked out of a job that I had for five years, and after being married for twenty-two years, got a divorce. That same year someone who I completely trusted and loved deceived me. Needless to say, the year was an extremely difficult one and I was hoping for something positive that would help me end it on a different note.

I decided to go back home to Nicaragua and join the rest of my extended family for a reunion. The political situation in the country had been dangerous for a long time. Rebels had taken over the country back in 1979, and everything had changed politically. But after years of oppression, the communist Sandinistas had been voted out of power. The civil war had ended, but the political intrigue continued and danger still existed. We were having a family reunion and my brothers and sister from different parts of the country flew in.

One morning, we all left the city and went to my father's ranch to spend the day. After riding horses, eating, drinking, and having a good time we left the ranch late, violating a city curfew that began at 6:00pm. It was dangerous to violate the curfew because the rebels came out at night. They traveled in big groups and coming into contact with them was not a desirable thing. By the time we left the ranch, it was already dark and I was driving with my brother, Justy, who was next to me on the passenger's seat. Justy was intoxicated and passed out as we began our journey back to town. I was in the driver's seat and the rest of my family was in two other vehicles about one kilometer ahead of us.

Clelia SantaCruz - LMSW

As we came off of a side road and made a right turn onto the main road leading to our city, I saw what I believed were at least a dozen rebels coming out of the bushes from both sides of the road about 70 yards from us. They had on their camouflage uniforms and had covered their noses and mouths with bandanas. They were armed with machine guns and motioned me to stop. I kept on driving very slowly, seeing them at a distance. Terrified and not knowing what to do, I woke my brother up and screamed, "Look at all those men, they came out of the bushes and are blowing their whistles, telling me to stop! What do I do?" He said a few bad words and told me to keep going because they were going to kill us anyway, but if I stopped, they were going to rape me, take everything from me, and then kill us. I was not excited about any of those choices and I made the decision to drive fast and not look back. I remember putting my hands on my head as if to cover it from the bullets that I thought were coming. They whistled again and I kept on driving and ignoring their order to stop. I remember saying the name of Jesus and knowing that we were going to die. My children's faces came to my mind, they were not on that trip with me and for a few seconds I was terrified to think that I would never see them again. To my surprise, the guerrilleros did not fire their guns, my head was still intact, and they did not follow us! As I passed them and ignored their call, I sped up as if I were getting out of hell. I knew that their bullets could have reached me, but I was not about to let them do the things that my brother said that they would do.

Two years earlier, one of my cousins had been in the same predicament. He was stopped by the rebels and did not follow their orders; he kept going and was killed. People say that his vehicle was unrecognizable from all of the bullets in it. It was a horrible experience for my family to know that a young, smart, and successful person was killed for absolutely nothing. He lived in the States and worked for the United Nations. He had a great future ahead of him. He was visiting his parents and lost his life because he failed to stop for the guerrilleros who have no value for life and are power hungry.

I don't know what those men saw in my vehicle, but I truly believe that they must have seen angels protecting us. No one could believe that they let us get away without harming us. My brother was so intoxicated that he would not have known if anything had happen to us. When we got back to the city and told the story to the rest of our family, I knew that it was a miracle and I praised God. His presence had saved our lives.

I was not walking closely with God at the time of that incident; I had just gone through a divorce and my life was pretty much a mess. I had made bad decisions and was reaping the consequences of my actions. I should have given my life right back to Christ after that incident, but instead I continued to try to make things better on my own and continued to fail miserably. Looking back, I know that God had a plan for me. I knew that eventually I was going to understand. Nothing works without Him. I finally got it and at this stage of my life, the only thing that I want to do is to serve Him and do His will. I am thirsty for His presence and His grace overwhelms me.

My husband and I were vacationing couple of years ago and were privileged to be on a beautiful beach. No one was around and we decided to go for a long walk and climb the huge rocks that would take us to the ocean on the other side. It took us over one hour to go around a cove and then we found some great rocks to lie on and do some meditation. During our walk, we had passed a young boy who seemed to be by himself. He appeared to be following us and I made a comment to my husband that he was probably a little pervert, just trying to see if we were getting away to be intimate with each other. As we went around the cove, we did not see the boy anymore. We don't know much about tides and noticed that the ocean was getting a little fuller, but did not think about it. We proceeded to relax and spend time listening to the waves and the awesome power of the water.

Forty-five minutes later, we realized that the water was getting very close to us. When we looked at the path that we had taken to get to the huge rocks that we were laying on, we realized that the path was covered with water and the waves seemed to be furious. We began to panic because there was no way to get back. We had huge rocks behind us and a huge ocean in front of us. Soon the water would overtake us and there would be no way out. We began to walk back through the rocks, and since they were covered with water and the waves were getting more and more violent, they became very slippery. We could not hold on and were falling with every step that we took. I began to pray in the Spirit and knew that somehow we were going to make it. Alex could not help me; he could barely help himself! We looked around the corner and all of sudden there was the little boy who we had seen before. He came out of nowhere to help us! He didn't even ask if we needed help, he just grabbed my hand and helped me walk on the slippery rocks. He never slipped and it was as if he had glue on the bottom of his feet. He took my hand and soon I was safe on the other side. Alex had managed to follow us and we were so glad that we had made it out alive.

Alex and I looked at each other and thought the exact same thing! Who was this little boy who came from out of nowhere just in time to help us? The boy said that his uncle was fishing somewhere, but we never saw him. We gave him all the money that we had and thanked him for being there in the right place at the right time. We had angels among us! God never ceases to amaze me in the ways that he shows up to help those who ask for His help. I truly believe that He has saved my life several times because I need to complete my assignment on this earth. I also believe that God has spared my brother's life numerous times. After many accidents and incidents, my brother has finally given his life to Christ and has changed his life completely.

My brother, Justy, had an issue with alcohol and his drinking created many negative situations in his life. I believed that God could change his circumstances and have a personal relationship with him. I knew that Jesus could heal him and restore his body and soul. Justy became very ill last year and many people did not think that he was going to make it. He had spent most of his life drinking heavily and had developed diabetes. He had also developed a condition where every inch of his body hurt incredibly. He could not sit, stand, or lie down without excruciating pain. I visited him early last year and prayed for his condition. Several family members were also praying.

Our Powerful Words

My aunt Vilma resides in the same city as Justy and she is a strong woman of faith. She would take Justy to every church meeting and he would allow her to take him. My mother was also praying for him daily, as I was. Every morning I would wake up and thank the Lord for giving my brother a pain-free day. I would thank God for bringing Justy closer to Him and for making a change in his life.

During the same year, I became ill and the doctors told me that I had to completely change my diet and several aspects of my life because there was very little that they could do to alleviate my pain. They scheduled a surgery because there was a small chance that it would help. Like my brother, I was in pain everyday, but with an entirely different condition.

With all of the prayers being poured into his life, Justy began to get better and in August, 2006, he came to California to do post-graduate studies in artificial insemination. He had finally returned to work as a Veterinarian and we were so excited to know that he was getting his life back on track. He had always been brilliant in his profession and even though at times he drank excessively, people loved him and respected him tremendously.

While Justy was in California, I called him several times and he stated that he was feeling great. He had quit drinking completely and was very aware that God had given him a miracle and an opportunity to make a difference. It was obvious to those of us who had to battle with him for his recovery. I was incredibly touched by his healing and I began to cry and thank God again for the miracle. It gave me faith to release my own pain to Him and when I did, He also touched my body! Two years have passed since that day when I cried out to God and thought that if I had that much faith about my brother's healing, I could also believe for myself. I cancelled the surgery, which was scheduled for September, 2006.

I have continued to eat all the foods that I love to eat, and I am healed! Seeing my brother's life radically changed and seeing his awareness that God gave him his healing, helped me to realize that if we have faith and a grateful heart, God can touch us and heal our bodies and minds. Discomfort comes once in a while, but I immediately remind my body that I am healed and that no spirit of pain will have power over me. I believe that we need to exercise our faith and remind the spirit of sickness that Jesus died so that we could have health and our sins could be forgiven.

Our Powerful Words

> "There is no greater joy nor greater reward than to make a fundamental difference in someone's life."
>
> *-Sister Mary Rose McGeady*

> "What is beautiful is not always good, but what is good is always beautiful."
>
> *-Unknown*

Chapter 22

There Are No Accidents
A Vision From God

How do we know when God talks to us? That is a question that we have all asked others and ourselves. Not long ago, I was talking to my sister and she innocently asked, "How do you know it is God?" I responded that the project that I was talking to her about was something that I would not ever want to do, but it would benefit others, therefore it had to be from Him. Many thoughts and ideas run through our minds and it is difficult to discern where they come from. Some might be from God; others are from our own desires or ambitions. I truly believe that God speaks to all of us about the things that He wants us to do. I wish there were a master plan somewhere that we could receive when we are born, but it does not work that way. The master plan exists, it is in His Word, but we have to find it. We can read the Bible and clearly see what He intends for us, and what our purposes are on this earth. We live here temporarily and our citizenship is not from this world, but in our short stay on this planet, we are supposed to fulfill our purposes. When God speaks, some of us hear Him and some of us don't. The more time that we spend in His presence, the easier it is to distinguish His voice.

Last December, I wanted to help someone in need during the Christmas holidays. There are plenty of organizations that need money for one thing or another, but I wanted to find someone specific who maybe needed some extra help that year. A few days later, I began to think of a family that I had met earlier that summer. I only saw the family once when I had interviewed them over a child abuse case that I was working on. The family had very little financial means and lived in a gang-infested part of town. Six months had passed by and I could not remember their names unless I went through a list of all the cases that I had worked for the past six months, which was something I did not want to do.

A couple of weeks went by, and the woman's face kept coming to my mind. I told the Lord that if it was Him talking to me about this family, then He somehow needed to help me remember who they were in order for me to find a number or address to contact them. He did! Somehow I came across the court report that I had written about the family and I was amazed to find it because I had not been looking for it. I knew then that God was really talking to me about giving this family a gift. By now, Christmas had come and gone and I was very busy with my own personal business. Everyday, the woman's face would come to my mind as I was going to sleep or during a time where I could not do much about it. The next morning I would forget again and would not remember again until I was in bed. I kept saying to the Lord, "I am so sorry; I will take care of it!"

Well, I began to experience car trouble and was forced to take my car to the dealership, which was close to where the family resided. I dropped the car off at the dealer the next day and my husband picked me up. I casually mentioned that I needed him to take me to the family's home. Alex was not very happy about my request and said that he just wanted to get home. I told him that I really needed to go by there because I had to give them some money. He asked why I owed them money and I said that I did not owe anything to them, but that God had asked me to take some money to them. I began to pray quietly and asked God to talk to Alex about it; he did not want to drive to that side of town even though we were not that far. A few minutes later, Alex asked me for the address and I was happy to give it to him. God had talked to him and he was ready to drive me to the family's home. He asked me if I had called them to make sure that they would be home when we arrived. I told him that their phone had been disconnected. Alex said a few negative things, but drove me to the house.

When we got there, I knocked on the door and the woman answered. I could see the family around the kitchen table, but they could not see me. I told the woman that I had no idea why I was there, but that God had placed her in my heart and I asked her if there was anything going on in her life. Her eyes became teary and she said that she was experiencing a very bad time and was contemplating suicide. She said that gang members had killed her son a few months earlier. She spoke about her son and told me that he was a good boy and that she had no idea why gang members would do such a thing. She said that she could not live without him and was having a very difficult time accepting his death. The woman had three more children under the age of twelve. The son who was killed was seventeen years old.

Immediately I knew why I was there and became overwhelmed with emotion. I began to speak about her son as if I knew what I was saying. It was as if I could see the boy in paradise! I told her that her son was in heaven, and that he wanted to tell her that he was fine and that she needed to be happy for him because he was not suffering anymore. I said that he wanted to see her smile and rejoice for him. I said that she needed to be strong for her other children and to let him go because he was with God. We were both crying at this time. I gave her the money that I had intended to give her, but I knew that my visit was not about money, but about a message that God had for her. I went back to the truck and Alex had witnessed part of our interaction from a distance. I was very emotional and felt that God had been speaking to me about giving hope to this woman and I had taken so much time to do it. Alex and I cried on our way home because we were so touched by God. If I had dismissed God's instruction, I would have missed the tremendous blessing to give that woman hope. I have discovered that nothing feels better than doing something good for others!

The Bible tells us that God knew us before we were in the womb. It is difficult to understand why he placed us with certain families and in a specific period of time. I have heard some people say that they wish that they had been born in the 1930s and others, in the 80's. I believe that I was born exactly at the perfect time that God created for me. Everything I have gone through in my life has prepared me for where I am today. I have made many mistakes, but I believe that they were part of the process. I do believe that there are mistakes that we make that slow down our ultimate destination, but eventually we will get to where we are supposed to be if we have a relationship with God and follow His guidance.

God designed us in such a way that we can only find true meaning in life when He is at the center of it. He desires intimacy with us and, being spirits ourselves, we are not truly satisfied until we have intimacy with Him. We crave meaning and try to find it in our jobs and earthly relationships, but we are never truly complete until we figure out that we are here for a purpose higher than ourselves. I have talked throughout this book about the void that I felt my whole life that did not go away until I developed a deep relationship with the Holy Spirit. When I truly began to seek Him, I saw opportunities and situations before me that were not accidents. They were there for a reason and I began to search for the meaning of what I thought that God was saying to me.

Paul, in his letter to the Philippians, talks about imitating Christ's humility and says that we should look not only to our own interest, but also to the interest of others. Looking at other people's interest had not been a priority in my life. I cared about people, but only those close to my heart. God had other plans and several years ago He began to do a work in me that has changed the direction of my life completely.

As I said in my introduction, I have had a desire to write a book for many years, but I had a lot of growing to do before I could reach my goal. When God gives us a vision, is not always at the most convenient time. I heard someone preach about the great potential in an unwanted calling and I have never understood that until now.

Our Powerful Words

Ever since I was a child, I have had vivid, repetitive dreams about particular things in my life. Some dreams I have understood, others I just tossed out and tried not to analyze, but for two solid years, I had dreams about children. At the beginning, I thought that I wanted to have a grandchild. My oldest son was twenty-six years old at the time and I thought that maybe unconsciously I wanted him to settle down and have a family. The dreams continued and they were so vivid that they began to concern me. I prayed about them and felt that God somehow wanted me to impact children's lives. My desire for many years has been to teach others about the power of our words and how what we say about our circumstances can change our destiny. When the dreams continued night after night, I thought that maybe God wanted me to teach children this concept so that when they grew up, they could have a closer relationship with Him and have a more successful life. I told the Lord that I did not understand why He was talking to me about children since I am not the kind person who likes to work with them. They are noisy, needy, and messy and I have had little patience with them. My sons are grown men now and I absolutely adore them and I enjoyed raising them, but I have only liked my own kids and never have been the kind of person who likes other children or who has patience with them.

A few months prior to the dreams, I was working out and riding my bike on a local trail, when the thought about impacting children entered my mind. After entertaining the thought for a few minutes, I realized what I was doing and quickly dismissed the thought. I love to talk to God when riding my bike or walking on the trail and since I was meditating on His word, it occurred to me that maybe He was speaking to me about the subject. I had dismissed the thought a couple of times, but it kept coming back to my mind and I told the Lord, "I know you are not talking to me about children. Why would you want me to have anything to do with kids? You know that they get on my nerves." I continued with my ride, but the thoughts did not go away and I said, "Well...if you are speaking to me, then show me something that is related to children and then I will know that it is actually from you and not from my demented mind."

Clelia SantaCruz - LMSW

Many times we ask God for a sign and that only shows our lack of faith. We might then see something and immediately think that the sign is from God, and it could be, but many times it is not. We should not be like Thomas and ask for evidence. We should have faith and know that if we begin to desire to help others without hidden motives, then it's from God! I continued to ride my bicycle and as I was crossing a street, a van with huge letters saying "Day Care Center" was parked right in front of me. I thought, "You have got to be kidding me! You are speaking to me! What would you want me to do with children? I can't have a childcare center, I would commit suicide!"

I came home and was upset about the whole incident and told my husband that I thought that God was talking to me about doing something with children. He looked at me and laughed. I told him that I had no idea what God was talking about and that He was going to have to get my attention some other way. My husband laughed because he knew that working with little ones would be the last thing in this world that I would want to do. He said, "Well you know that God has a sense of humor, especially when it comes to you." I thought, "That is very funny, hon, but I am not thinking about it anymore." I put the thought of working with children in the back of my mind and forgot about it.

The dreams did not start that night, but came soon after. I had forgotten about my bike ride, therefore as the dreams began and got more intense, it took me longer to see the connection. Many times I would have the same exact dream every night. I would dream that a little girl would be with me and I would give her lots of affection. I would take care of her and other kids who were around. I did not see faces, but the little girl was always there among other children.

The first few dreams, as I said before, did not surprise me and I really thought that it was just my desire to be a grandmother. Maybe I was experiencing empty nest syndrome. My youngest son, Josh, had moved away to college and maybe just maybe I was melancholic about not having him in my life each day. When Josh moved out, I really thought that I was prepared, but when he drove off, I was overwhelmed with sadness about my precious little boy growing up. It was the beginning of another stage in my life and I realized that life was not going to be the same. I later found that the dreams had nothing to do with Josh moving away from home or about Eddie giving me a grandchild.

The little girl in my dream started to haunt me night after night. In my dream I would take care of her, but I knew that she was not mine. She belonged to somebody else, but her parents were not around. I would wake up and ask God, "What is this? ... I am going crazy with the same dream every night; what are you trying to tell me?" It became clear to me that He wanted me to be involved in something related to children. I kept asking Him for more signs and He would give them to me, but they were nothing that I could decipher because I was not allowing myself to accept what I thought He was asking of me. I would ask Him again, "Are you sure that you are talking to me? You probably have the wrong person; I am telling you that I have no desire to work with children, I don't even like them!"

The dreams continued and I remembered the bike ride conversation that I had had with God. I thought, "Oh NO ... You are talking to me again about that daycare center!" Running a day care center would be a nightmare to me and I had no idea how to go about it. I put it out of my mind again, hoping that He would forget, but He didn't.

At this point I was almost positive that He wanted me to work with children or at least have some kind of influence, though He knows well that in all of my years of counseling, I have chosen not to work with them. He knows very well that I just wanted to buy some property in the ocean, build a beautiful home, and write books. As the vision became clearer, I realized that not only does He want me to work with little children, but He also wants me to feed the elderly, which is another population that in all of my years of counseling, I have chosen not to work with. During the same time when I was trying to decipher the children dreams, I figured out that I was somehow to impact elderly people. I was shocked!

Clelia SantaCruz - LMSW

At that time, my grandmother was very sick and did not have much time left. She was dying and had been transported to a nursing home. My aunt Lucy, who loved her dearly, was at the nursing home taking care of her each day. I did not have much of a relationship with the only grandmother who I ever had, because she never had time for me when I was growing up. She would come over to visit my mother, but never had a kind word for me. She moved to Texas with Lucy when she was about forty-five years old and when I moved to Texas, I began to get to know her. I did not see her often and did not bond with her like a child would bond with a grandmother; deep inside I resented her for not being available for me while I was growing up and starving for love and attention. At the age of eighty-three, she was now dying in a nursing home. When I visited her, I would pass by the rooms of other patients who appeared to be extremely lonely and sick. No one came to visit them, no one showed concern. My grandmother was blessed to have my aunt Lucy taking care of her 24/7, but others did not have anyone. I began to feel pain in seeing these lonely, elderly people. It would break my heart to pass by those rooms and I began to wonder why I was experiencing those feelings.

I had many opportunities to work with elderly patients in my career as a counselor, but turned down the offers every time as I had no desire to work with them. Somehow elderly people scared me, because it made me face the reality that we are not going to make it out of here alive. Older people are close to the end of the journey and apparently they brought me in touch with feelings that I did not want to have. Getting old meant reaching the end of the journey and having to answer to God for things that we did or did not do which was a thought that I did not want to entertain in my mind.

As I think back, I believe that I knew that God wanted to use me somehow for many years. I had preachers prophesy over me, but I never took it seriously. I did not want to accept that God might want to use me; I was too selfish to think about anyone else. I did not know it then, but God was changing my heart little by little and placing in me the desire to make a change. At that point in my life, I had no idea of the level or how to even go about it. My questions to God were the same,

Our Powerful Words

"Are you sure that you are talking to me? I never wanted to work with these people." Well, our plans are not always His plans and after many nights of having dreams about children, I had one that impacted me the most. I saw a little child in my arms who was drowning in a bathtub while I was bathing her. My hands were slippery with soap, and the child fell out of my hands and was submerged under water. I tried to pull her out of the small tub, but my slippery hands would lose her again.

The first time that I had that dream, I woke up and was terrified. The next night I had another vivid dream. This time I was inside someone's home and looking out to their back yard. I saw children outside in something that appeared to be like a fenced pigpen. I asked a woman inside the house to bring the children in, because they appeared to be cold and hungry. The woman told me not to worry; they could not feel the cold. She said that they were like animals and were used to being outside and needed nothing. I screamed and said, "You can't do that, they are children and have feelings...Bring them in!" I woke up from that horrible dream and I was sweaty, completely awake, and unable to go back to sleep.

After the last two dreams I told my husband that I could not take it anymore, I was concerned about the dreams and needed to talk to someone about them. Alex believed that I was not crazy and we both began to pray about the issue. He never doubted that I was hearing from God and we both decided that we would be obedient to His word no matter what our flesh was telling us to do.

The year before the dreams started, my husband and I had taken a trip to my country, Nicaragua. I wanted Alex to meet my father and see where I came from. We had interest in buying ocean-front property and made the decision to spend a couple of weeks visiting different places. One day as we were out eating dinner at a restaurant, my heart was touched when we saw kids begging for food and selling jewelry and nick knacks to support their parents. One nine-year-old child told us that she could not go home empty handed, or her mother would beat her up. We bought jewelry from her, and I was very upset to know of the abuse that goes on with the children in that country. We came back to the States and soon after, the dreams began. But I did not put it together until much later. The connection was not clear, but one day it all of a sudden became crystal.

After experiencing a civil war that lasted many years, Nicaragua is currently the second poorest country in the western hemisphere. The poverty is incredible and the needs innumerable. Little by little, the whole vision began to unfold and God placed in my heart a vision to build an orphanage. The orphanage was to have two separate wings that connected in the middle where the kitchen and dining room would be. One wing would house functioning elderly who do not require intense medical supervision. In Nicaragua, the government does not have a social security program to help the elderly. If they don't have family to care for them, then they are forced to beg on the streets and live in cardboard homes. There are what they call "elderly asylums" where they can live, but space is limited and food is scarce. They live from contributions given by citizens and believe me, contributions don't come often.

In my vision, the other wing would house children, from infants to age fourteen. Our biggest need – whether young or old – is to feel connection, touch, affection, and what better way to give it to both young and old, than to put them together. The alpha and the omega, the beginning and the end of our lives right there to meet each other's needs. Little children can give love and affection to the elderly and they in turn can give the same to children. After having that vision, I knew that it had to be from God because there was no way that I would have thought about it on my own.

In 2004, Alex and I made plans to go to Nicaragua and see if a movement from God was going on there. We knew that if we were obedient, God would show us the next step. I am sure that it was difficult for my husband to tell people that we were going to another country to look for land to build an orphanage based on a dream that his wife was having. But people who knew us and knew our relationship with God believed that we were following the steps to our vision. Others probably thought that we had gone insane; one of my brothers was included in the last group. Knowing that I needed to do something about it did not give me clarity about how to do it. I had no idea how to go about making an impact in that country because I knew I did not have the funds to build an orphanage/elderly asylum.

As I finish this book in 2008, we have seen an enormous amount of movement in Nicaragua. It appears that when God speaks to us, he speaks to all of us. Some of us listen, some of us don't, but God will do what He intends for us to do. There is a revival going on in Nicaragua right now, but when He first placed the thought in my mind, there was not much going on there. Everywhere I go today, I hear of some church or some group participating in some kind of mission there. The government has some programs to help autistic children, but thousands of children without special needs are being severely abused and no one is doing anything about it because there is no place to take them. They can take the children away from abusive parents, but they have no place to house them.

Alex and I decided to talk to some of our friends at church about our lack of funds and they suggested that we talk to different people. We did and interest was shown, but nothing ever manifested. While trying to figure out what to do, we could see the hand of God. Some of the experiences that we encountered were incredible and we knew that we were on the right path. We spoke to a man of God named Bob Mason, who is the founder of Missions International. He has helped to build churches and orphanages all over the globe. We met with him briefly in October of 2004, and he suggested that we make an appointment and talk to him more about our vision. With the holidays approaching and the business of life, we put our meeting in the back of our minds and it was not until my dreams came to be so vivid that I called Bob Mason.

I first communicated with Clayton Phillips, who was working closely with Bob and to my surprise, he said that we had been in their minds. We meet with Clayton and Bob, and Bob suggested that we take a trip to Nicaragua to find land in order to begin the project. We prayed about it and Bob believed that God was communicating with us and would show us the way. We prayed that there would be someone in

Nicaragua with the same vision. Someone who would want to impact children and would have the resources to donate the land. Well…that is exactly what happened! I was amazed at the way that everything worked out. The Holy Spirit was at work the entire time! It gave us chills to see God's perfect timing.

The first few days were spent in a town named Esteli, which I thought was a good place for the orphanage. My mother moved back to Nicaragua a few years ago and settled in that city. I thought that it could be a good place because she could check on things for us. Once the orphanage was built, mother could make sure that the resources would be distributed honestly and that the kids would be taken care of.

We met with the mayor of that city and he was very open and willing to help us in any way that he could. He promised to find the best place available for my vision. The mayor was a known Sandinista. (Sandinistas were the rebels who overthrew the democratic government that existed twenty-nine years ago). I told him that I was not interested in politics and that I would not give any credit to the government because I did not believe in Sandinism. I explained to him that my vision was from God and that we did not want anything to do with the Sandanistas. His response amazed me; he said that he had found Christ and that he really cared about doing the right thing for the community. We talked about Jesus and witnessed to each other. Our meeting ended on a good note, and we told him that we had to pray about it and would let him know after returning to the States. When we left his office, we felt as if things were moving too quickly. We had two additional weeks there and we were surprised to find that our work for God was done. We decided to enjoy our next two weeks, but felt uneasy, as if something else were coming.

The next day, we decided to go spend a few days by the ocean in San Juan Del Sur, a beautiful place about seventeen miles from the coast of Costa Rica. My dream has always been to buy property by the ocean, write books, and of course live happily ever after. We had no intention of buying property during this trip; we did not have the money. I had taken off the entire past year to complete this book and had been living off of my savings. It was not a good time to spend money on anything, much less property.

While eating lunch at a restaurant on the beach, we asked a woman who was sitting at the next table to take our picture. I have no problem speaking to strangers and quickly asked her where she was from and what she was doing there. The questions turned into a four-hour meeting where we shared everything from God to politics and psychology. She and her friend were looking for ocean-front property, and when I told them that we had been looking the previous year, she shared all of the information that she had about different places and different prices. Prior to meeting us, they had planned to eat a quiet lunch and go look at property that they had seen a few months earlier. They invited us to follow them so that we could see what a great deal they were going to get.

We followed them to see a beautiful piece of land on a mountain that overlooked the ocean. They found that the price that they were given six months prior had completely sky rocketed and they were very disappointed that they had not invested when they had the chance. We told them that we were sorry about their loss and that we had to get back to our hotel. We were planning to leave the wonderful beach town and head to the north of the county where my father lived. We told them to let us know if they found a good deal, because we were going to be around for a few more hours. We exchanged hotel information with our new friends and said goodbye.

A couple of hours later as we were leaving the hotel, we were told at the front lobby that we had a message from our friends. They had found another piece of property and left a message saying that we "must" see it. Alex and I didn't know how we were going to hook up with them again, because we were getting ready to eat dinner and did not have cell phones. We put our suitcases in our rental car, and had started to drive off when we saw them walking toward us. They told us everything about the property and we decided to follow them again to look at it. We loved the property; it was a beautiful resort with a private beach. Water and mountains were all around us and we fell in love with God's creation. We then remembered that the reason for our trip was not about us, but about the vision that God had given to us. We did not have any money to buy property and did not understand why we were wasting our time looking.

We left our friends at the resort and told them that we were going back to town and would probably eat dinner at the same restaurant where we had met them earlier. They stayed behind at the resort, talking to the owner and we thought that we would never see them again.

While eating dinner at the same restaurant, we looked up and there were our new friends coming our way. They were looking for us and wanted to spend a little more time with us. We greeted them and proceeded to enjoy each other's company again. About twenty minutes later, the son of the owner of the property we had looked at earlier named Hector, walked in and recognized us. He asked if he could join us and we invited him to sit at our table. We began to talk and he seemed fascinated by my profession and the topic of psychology. We talked about our life philosophies and during the conversation, Alex and I mentioned our vision to have an orphanage somewhere in Nicaragua. To our surprise, he said that his father had had a similar vision and that we had to meet him in order to tell him ours. Hector told us that his father was the owner of 4,000 acres where a resort was being created, but that he had always wanted to do something for the community and to change young people's mentality. He asked us to stay an extra day and talk to him about our philosophy and our vision.

We had our suitcases in the car and were planning to leave after dinner and drive four hours to my dad's town. We hoped that someone would offer us property close to my dad's ranch. My father owns lots of land, but his properties would be our last resort as they are not as close to the city, as we desired. We wanted to have choices of where to build the orphanage according to the various needs of specific cities. We told Hector that we were not sure about staying an extra night, but he continued to urge us to meet his father. He offered us a free night at his resort, and since we had seen how beautiful it was, the decision to stay

Our Powerful Words

became easier. Hector wanted us to get up in the morning, walk the beach, enjoy the view, and eat breakfast with his father.

We stayed at the resort and it was beautiful and peaceful. We could see every star in the sky and falling asleep while listening to the sound of the ocean was heaven. The next morning, Hector knocked at our door about 9am. We had just returned from a wonderful walk where we were able to meditate and spend time with God, laying on a rock, hearing the ocean waves, and admiring God's awesome creation. Hector had invited us to eat breakfast with him and his father and then take a ride to look at what his father had done with his own personal vision. After breakfast, we got into the father's vehicle and took off to the top of the mountain. He revealed to us that he had had a vision of educating children and teaching them about God. He wanted to provide shelter, education, and medical and dental services for children. He said that we could share in his vision or create our own. He was willing to do whatever we wanted and he would support us by giving us the land. I asked how much land he could provide and his response was, "As much you need." We felt chills going down our bodies and after talking more at length about our vision, we said that we would have to pray about it because this vision was God's and not ours.

When we got back, we were still amazed about the movement of God while in Nicaragua and our faith increased tremendously. My son contacted me a few days later to let me know that his roommate, Kevin, had gone to Louisiana with his girlfriend and that Kevin had met a man at a family gathering. The man was talking about Nicaragua and Kevin overheard him speaking about it. He approached him and said that his roommate's mother had just gotten back from that country and was looking for land for an orphanage. They began to talk and the man gave him his business card so that he could give it to me. He informed Kevin that he was born and raised in Nicaragua. He was an architect practicing in Louisiana and he offered to help us if we needed help with the plans for the building. He also mentioned that his sister had an orphanage in Nicaragua and that he goes yearly to take toys for the children. I thought that it had to be from God for Kevin to meet this man in another state, especially since he was just visiting and attending the gathering with the young lady who he was dating.

To my amazement, this particular gentleman and I began to e-mail each other and during one of the e-mails, he mentioned that he was half Chinese and half Nicaraguan. I told him that I have family members who are very close to me who are also half Chinese. My father's sister, Vilma, married a Chinese gentleman many years ago and now I have wonderful Chinese and Hispanic cousins. I mentioned their last name and told him some specifics about the family. He returned my email saying, "Wow, it is a small world." He told me that my cousins are related to him, they are his first cousins also. He told me that he spent summers at their family ranch and loved to be around them. He has wonderful memories of the times spent with the family.

It is a small world and God has a sense of humor; there I was in Texas and I came into contact with this man through my son's roommate and then he just happened to be a cousin-in-law? With God, there are no accidents. When we ask Him to open doors and place people into our lives or remove people from our path who are not supposed to be there, He does. That specific prayer has been a daily prayer for me. I not only pray it for my husband and myself, but I also pray it for my children, my entire extended family, and even my friends. One of my daily affirmations is that I have favor with people and I believe in my heart that God has given me favor, it shows up in my life each day.

The orphanage is a God-sized assignment and it will require a tremendous amount of faith to carry it out. I don't know why he would choose my husband and I for such an assignment, but we will do whatever it takes to see that we carry out what God has placed in our hearts. We have met people who are willing to help build, but it is taking much longer than I thought that it would take. I am praying that God continues to give me a clear vision of the next step. Never in my life would I have thought that I could impact children and the elderly. Never in my life would I have thought that God could use me for anything. I have messed up so many things in my life. I have been self-centered and only involved with my own agenda. God is so amazing that

Our Powerful Words

He loves me and has been preparing me to carry out such a big assignment. I don't want to let Him down and I already feel that I have as it has taken me so long to finish this book. Satan has been working over-time to keep me down and has thrown all kinds of things my way – from doubt, to conflict, to illnesses, to fear. I believe that this book is somehow tied to the assignment ahead of me in Nicaragua.

I took another trip to Nicaragua in 2005, and I began to feed the elderly at a nursing home. I am committed to start with that until I am able to raise the money that I need to build the orphanage/elderly asylum. While visiting the country again, I went to take pictures of kids and the elderly so that I would have something to show here in the States. I wanted the Lord to open up the door so that I could speak in churches, tell my vision, and promote this book. After days of driving around the country and going into villages and different places to take pictures, I went to visit my brother, Justy. He had been extremely ill and everyone kept saying that he would not last the rest of the year. After spending a couple of days with him and praying for his healing, I packed my bags and took them to the car. Breakfast was ready and I was called to come and eat with him before leaving town. I left my bags inside my car, which I had parked right outside of his house. After finishing breakfast, I hugged him and his wife and said, "Goodbye." To my surprise, someone had broken into my car and stolen my bag with my two cameras full of videos and pictures that I had taken for two weeks. I felt a horrible pain in my heart. I went into the house and began looking for my camera bag, hoping that maybe I had left it somewhere inside. Everyone in the house was looking for it, but the bag was gone.

My brother said that there had been lots of robberies going on, and that burglars had recently taken some expensive equipment out of his truck. He suggested that I go to the radio station and announce that we would give a reward if the cameras were returned. I did and it was announced all over town that someone had stolen my cameras. My niece and I went to several pawnshops and looked to see if someone had taken them there. No one knew anything, no one had seen anything. I went by the police station, filled out a report, and paid a policeman to go around the small town with me to every camera store and even to the Mercado where they sell all kinds of things. After several hours of frantically searching for my cameras that contained two weeks worth of work, I just wanted to cry and scream – and I did.

I left the town and drove to my mother's town three hours away. During the entire trip, I cried and told the Lord that I did not know how in the world something like that had happened. I questioned my vision and blamed Him for not keeping something like that from happening. I told him that I was trying to do His work and it was apparent to me that He did not want me to do it anymore. I wanted to know why He was wasting my time if He was not willing to help me. After crying and talking and yelling for over two hours, I stopped my car, rested my head on the steering wheel, and cried some more. I got out of the car to stretch and was surrounded by mountains and green pastures. I could see the awesomeness of His creation. I told Him that I did not understand, and that He just needed to give me peace. I had taken a trip with the pure intention of gathering pictures and information to do the vision that I thought that He had placed in my heart. A peace came over me and it was as if He was saying, "This is just another attack from Satan. Keep standing, for my grace is sufficient for you."

To this date, I don't understand why I went through that experience, but I do know that I have to continue pressing on to do the assignment that God has told me to do. Satan will flee if I resist him, but if I don't, he will continue to throw obstacles in my way and keep me from making a tremendous impact in the lives of children and the elderly who desperately need someone to care.

When I arrived at my mother's home, she was waiting for me and cried with me because she knew what it meant to lose both cameras. She gave me some encouraging words and told me that God would find another way. I left Nicaragua a few days later and I met a man who sat next to me on the plane. He was in Nicaragua on a mission trip. He and his wife help children in Guatemala and he was visiting my country as he had heard about the tremendous need to help children. He was a strong Christian and we talked throughout the entire flight about God and the mission field. He said that he had pictures that I could use, but I wanted my own pictures of children who I had spent time with. It was nice of him to offer the pictures, and I felt that God had placed an angel on the plane with me to let me know that He was in control. I don't know if I will ever see that men again or if we could ever work together to feed children. I think that his presence on that plane was so that I would know that God's vision was real and not let it die.

Last year, Bishop Dehart, a wonderful man of God who has dedicated his life to serving Christ, became interested in my vision. He is the Bishop of Heartland Church, in Irving, Texas, where Alex and I attend. He and his precious wife, Doris, went with me to Nicaragua to look at the land that given to us by Mr. Sanchez in San Juan Del Sur a few years ago. We visited with the developer, and after several hours of conversation, we left with mixed feelings about our meeting. We did not say anything to each other that day, but each one of us had a little doubt about that particular location being the best for our vision. While eating breakfast the next day, Bishop mentioned something about the meeting and we began to talk about our feelings. We felt as if the developer's intentions were not the same as ours. It really did not matter what intentions he had because he had promised to give us the land with no ties attached and we were to use it any way we wanted. But deep inside we could see that he probably would interfere somehow and that his intentions were to promote his own resort and look good doing a social project. We did not make any decisions and decided to each pray about the issue, knowing that God would give us the answer. I know how I felt during my first meeting with the developer and when the land was given to us and I know that God was in the middle of it. It was confusing that we were having second thoughts about it. I believe that God gives us glimpses of what He can do when we believe. Whether we build the orphanage there or not, I know that He was involved; the experiences that I have gone through could not have been accidents.

During our trip, we visited several areas of the country, including three orphanages where we obtained wonderful ideas about our project. The vision that God gave me several years ago has become extremely clear as far as the building and the people who we will serve. It is still not clear from where the funds are going to come, but I believe that God will make it happen.

As we were ready to return to the States, we decided to spend the night in Managua so that we would be closer to the airport the next day. I had made reservations at a local hotel across the street from the airport. When we arrived, we did not like the facility because it was under construction. We decided to look for a different place and were able to find room at a well-known American hotel. The next day while eating breakfast, we happened to sit next to a table full of missionaries from Costa Rica. They were laughing and speaking Spanish and I made a comment about a joke that one of them was telling. We began to talk to each other and found that they were in Nicaragua trying to help children. They agreed that the need in country was enormous! That touched our hearts and we knew that we were supposed to meet them. They gave us some information and we exchanged phone numbers. I felt as if I was experiencing another God moment!

As we left the restaurant and were walking to our rooms to get our suitcases, I ran into a friend of mine who I had not seen in thirty years. He was trying to get an appointment with the ambassador of China, who was apparently staying at the same hotel. We were shocked to see each other and could not stop hugging one another. I had grown up with him and knew his entire family well.

I told him what I was doing and introduced him to Lady Dee and Bishop. He promised to obtain some information that we needed and to talk to someone about donating land. Lady Dee and Bishop were touched by the "coincidence" and felt that it was one more thing to let us know that God was involved. If we had stayed at the other hotel, we would have never met the missionaries from Costa Rica or seen my friend! I don't know if these people will ever cross our paths again, but the fact that those meetings took place only reaffirms that we live in a small world controlled by something higher. God is in control!

Our Powerful Words

Having Bishop Dehart and Lady Dee involved in this project is a gift from above. I know that together we will do what God has placed in our hearts and that soon children who had no one to care for them and elderly who had been forgotten by others will have a place that they can call home.

Clelia SantaCruz - LMSW

About the Author

Clelia SantaCruz has served as a motivational counselor for couples and individuals for over fifteen years. Her mission is to encourage people to make positive changes in their lives by releasing their pain and issues to God. Clelia is in the process of building an orphanage and home for the elderly in Nicaragua, her country of origin. She currently resides in Colleyville, Texas with her husband, Alex and her youngest son, Josh.

Printed in the United States
133113LV00001BC/2/P